Booz Allen Hamilton, a global strategy and
technology consulting firm, works with clients
to deliver results that endure.

Booz Allen Hamilton:

Helping Clients Envision the Future

Art Kleiner

GREENWICH PUBLISHING GROUP, INC.
OLD SAYBROOK, CONNECTICUT

Booz | Allen | Hamilton
90 years delivering results that endure

Printed and bound in the United States of America. No part of
this publication may be reproduced or transmitted in any form
or by any means, electronic or mechanical, including photo-
copying, recording, or any information storage and retrieval
system now known or to be invented, without permission in
writing from Booz Allen Hamilton, 8283 Greensboro Drive,
McLean, VA 22102, except by a reviewer who wishes to
quote brief passages in connection with a review written for
inclusion in a magazine, newspaper, or broadcast.

Produced and published by Greenwich Publishing Group, Inc.
Old Saybrook, Connecticut
www.greenwichpublishing.com

Designed by Clare Cunningham Graphic Design

Library of Congress Control Number: 2004111918

ISBN: 0-944641-64-4

First Printing: November 2004

10 9 8 7 6 5 4 3 2 1

Any trademarks in this book are the property of their
respective owners.

Table of Contents

Preface: What Is Management Consulting?

We live today in a world driven by organizations. Our ability to live well depends on the quality and integrity of the businesses, governments, and other organizations that serve us. Their success, in turn, depends ever more on intangible assets such as information, services, and brand value.

Management consultants tend to be hired by organizations and their leaders to help them navigate the complexities of changing business and political landscapes—and thus to become more effective and successful. They draw on a broad base of professional and personal expertise: management theory, technology, psychology, and creativity combined with curiosity and eloquence. At their best, they apply the fresh perspective of a smart, trusted outsider to bring clients to the point of breakthrough and help them envsion the future.

I was asked to write this book because I have a background in writing about management thinking, but I had never before seen up-close the work, people, and values of a firm like Booz Allen Hamilton. Because the nature of the job changes frequently, as does the world, Booz Allen partners and employees have to be perpetual learners who reinvent the profession every day. One constant, however, is their overriding purpose: helping clients succeed.

But what does that mean on a day-to-day basis?

First, it means building long-term relationships predicated on trust and mutual respect. Some Booz Allen client relationships go back 40 or 50 years. The consultant is hired, however, to see past that familiarity: to locate and recognize the significant bits and patterns of data that lurk unheeded in reports and interviews and convert them into suggestions for action.

Working on a client's behalf means focusing not on being right or on impressing people but on producing results. People who become corporate officers, or "partners," of Booz Allen are typically those who see a job through to the end, judging the job not by the size of the fee paid but by the progress clients make (and, to be sure, by their willingness to hire Booz Allen again).

Hence the importance of honesty, objectivity, integrity, and transparency to management consulting. This is particularly apparent after the scandals of the Enron era, when ethical dilemmas at many firms came to light. Booz Allen people pride themselves on their independence and their resistance to co-optation or pressure. There are many stories in this book where consultants told clients the truth, even when it was difficult, uncomfortable, or impolitic.

Management consulting requires people with diverse backgrounds—in education, work experience, nationality, ethnicity, and perspective. Booz Allen has learned the value of applying a broad range of attitudes and resources to client engagements. This is an increasingly global profession, one that requires moving beyond the boundaries of nations while respecting the sovereignty and values of the cultures within them.

Largely because of this melting of national and industrial barriers, management consultants are bridge builders. This book tells how Booz Allen gradually discovered its own significant competitive advantage—its unique ability to combine seemingly incompatible types of work: strategic management consulting (as typically conducted for corporations) and technological implementation (as often required by government agencies).

In the course of writing this book, I've found that Booz Allen consultants share a kind of modesty. They don't take credit for their clients' success; rather they see themselves as witnesses to it. They don't steer the ships of state or commerce, yet in this complex, multifaceted world Booz Allen's consultants find themselves increasingly valued as navigators.

Their knowledge and perspectives were invaluable to me in this project, as were the encouragement and guidance of Booz Allen's 90th-anniversary book team—Marie Lerch, David Doty, and Amy Matthews—plus the help of my associate Emily Freidberg and the support of my own consulting team at home: Faith, Frances, Elizabeth, and Constance. Heartfelt thanks to them all and to the many others, too numerous to mention, without whom this book never could have been written.

—*Art Kleiner*

A Note About Confidentiality
Booz Allen Hamilton assures its commercial clients confidentiality; much of the firm's work for government agencies is a matter of public record. Certain clients have allowed the firm, in this book and other communication materials, to discuss work we have done on their behalf. Booz Allen is grateful for their cooperation.

Delivering Results that Endure

Booz Allen Hamilton is a global consulting company with expertise in strategy, organization and change leadership, operations, information technology, and technology management.

Based in McLean, Virginia, it is a private company owned by its officers, whose titles are vice president or senior vice president. They are listed and pictured at the back of this book. Because Booz Allen was formed and for much of its history was structured as a partnership, the officers are often called "partners," especially within the firm.

Booz Allen has evolved over the decades, and now two operating units have emerged as the main interfaces through which the firm serves its clients. The Worldwide Commercial Business (WCB) works with the world's leading corporations to enhance their long-term competitive advantage, often by helping them deal with multiple, seemingly conflicting objectives—reducing uncertainty and helping to manage risks by developing and implementing clear solutions. The Worldwide Technology Business (WTB) offers a broad range of management consulting, engineering, information-technology, and systems development/integration services to government agencies, institutions, and infrastructure organizations worldwide.

While it has two distinct business units, Booz Allen operates as one firm, applying its multifunctional expertise and capabilities to solve problems in both the commercial and public sectors—and often in engagements that bridge these once-separate realms. Whatever the market, Booz Allen's focus is on producing enduring results for institutions seeking to manage complexity and develop resilience in the face of constant change.

Foreword: Enduring Values, Enduring Institutions

Imagine Booz Allen Hamilton as a start-up. In 1914, on the eve of World War I, a young college graduate in psychology named Edwin G. Booz opened an office and went into business for himself. He was equipped with a set of new ideas about management. Going far beyond the era's prevailing mindset, Ed Booz believed passionately that he could help companies succeed by bringing them a human touch: expert, candid advice and an outside perspective on their businesses. To be sure, he would use sophisticated management techniques, but he insisted that "people, not products" were the focus of work. And he knew that placing the right person in the right position and giving him or her the best possible support would lead to better results than relying on any particular theory, method, or tool.

With that innovative approach, Ed Booz—working out of a two-room, rented office in Chicago—gave birth to the modern management consulting profession. And to this day, his core belief in finding good talent and embedding it in clients remains an essential quality of the company he founded.

If Ed Booz visited today, I am sure

that he would be very proud of how the firm has grown, and of the impact we've had on our clients and the world. We're a $2.7 billion company with 15,000 employees on six continents. We occupy a unique position as a consulting firm that implements as well as it thinks—with vitally strong capabilities in commercial and government work and the rare ability to integrate them. Most important, we have a reputation for operating successfully, responsibly, and ethically. This is priceless, especially at a time when the survival of many professional services firms has been challenged.

Ed would be especially proud of our people. In our role as consultants, we have been privileged to see, take part in, and catalyze many key events in the spheres of both business and government. We have been involved in the emergence of modern corporations in the 1920s and 1930s, the Allied mobilization in World War II, the beginning and end of the Cold War, the dawn of the Space Age, the evolution of the personal computer, the breakup of old telephone systems and the creation of new ones, early public-private sector work in the European Union, the emergence of

strong economies in Asia and South America, the waves of deregulation in the 1980s, the movement for environmental protection, and the birth of the modern U.S. National Football League. We have also been witness to or participant in the reunification of Germany, the Gulf Wars, the response to the terrorist attacks of 9/11, the rise and fall of business cycles, and dramatic shifts in the ways that commerce, war, and peace have been conducted.

Every day Booz Allen people deliver results that endure for the world's leading companies, institutions, and governments. Every day they make a difference beyond the walls of our clients' offices, too—through pro bono work addressing major problems such as the spread of HIV in the developing world. I believe Booz Allen Hamilton's people owe their success, and the firm its longevity, to the continued evolution and application of the values that Ed Booz established and subsequent managers nourished—client service, diversity, excellence, entrepreneurship, teamwork, professionalism, fairness, integrity, respect, and trust. Our continued success in the future will not depend just on bringing

our brains to our work, but on bringing our hearts—our spirit of service, our passions, and our deep ties to each other and our clients.

Deepening our awareness of ourselves and our world is one way to cultivate and enrich our collective intellect and heart. That's why we are publishing this book. Produced for Booz Allen Hamilton's 90th anniversary in 2004, it is not just a birthday celebration but an exploration of the history and future—of our firm, our profession, our community of clients, and of the evolving global civilization in which we live. Booz Allen is 90 years young because we take pride in our history but don't rest on laurels. We have remained true to our values and our tradition of excellence and client service yet have focused on the future and embraced change. How have we—and, more important, how have our clients—done that? Read on, for this book is the story of that remarkable journey.

—*Ralph W. Shrader, Ph.D.*
Chairman and Chief Executive Officer
October 2004

Establishing a Profession

Nineteen fourteen was not just the beginning of the first World War, the conflict that set the tone for the remainder of the century. It was a turning point in many other ways. The ideas of Sigmund Freud, William James, Friedrich Nietzsche, and Charles Darwin were ascending. Each, in his own way, spoke of a universe more progressive, more evolutionary, and more responsive to the influence of humankind.

The modern business organization—with owners separate from managers, and employees numbering in the hundreds instead of the tens or dozens—was less than 60 years old. Already, it had mobilized people and technology to produce unprecedented wealth, not just for owners but for consumers. The nature of government also was changing as smaller nations merged or expanded into larger and more complex nation-states, with new kinds of government agencies to run their administrations (and in some cases, empires).

Wilbur and Orville Wright, with their first successful flight in 1903, ushered in not just one of the defining inventions of the 20th century but an innovative new industry that made global organizations feasible. Shown here is one of the Wright brothers' first biplanes, built in 1911 and photographed in 1934 at Central Airport in Philadelphia for a celebration of the 31st anniversary of the aviation industry. Management consultants working for Booz Allen were among the first professionals to study the nature of the aviation industry.

E conomically, much of the world was mired in a mild recession, but people felt optimistic and a bit awestruck by the changes around them. The Panama Canal had opened only one year earlier. Miraculous new inventions like the electric light, the telephone, the automobile, and the motion picture were rapidly becoming commonplace. Only a few years before, two men had flown a motorized vehicle through the air in North Carolina. The mass-market magazine, then about 30 years old, and the plate-glass window, which allowed supermarkets and department stores to colorfully showcase consumer goods, had enabled a bold new profession called mar-

keting. That term first emerged in 1914 at Harvard's new business school, which had opened just six years before.

Northwestern University, a few miles north of Chicago, had no formal business school, but its faculty included Walter Dill Scott, one of the pioneering management academics of his time. Scott, then 45, was a professor of psychology. He had written the first books published in the United States on advertising practice (*Theory of Advertising,* 1903) and on advertising psychology (*Psychology of Advertising,* 1910). Scott understood the human component of business, not just in advertising but in all management. He was the first to write about

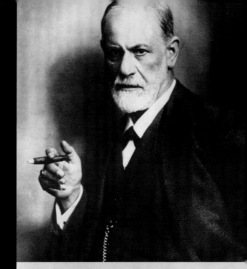

Innovations in technology and thinking were widespread in the years before World War I. Sigmund Freud and others revitalized psychology.

The automobile (Henry Ford's Model T is shown here) brought new mobility along with new mass-production methods that made the car affordable to hundreds of thousands of people. Inventors tapped electrons for sound and light, leading to the telephone, radio, sound recording, and the light bulb. Meanwhile, distribution of large quantities of goods and raw materials took place on the forerunners to today's giant container ships.

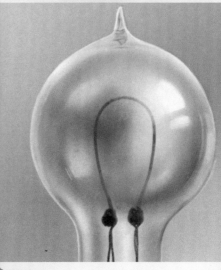

the way advertising could trigger deeply held emotions and instincts, and he scoffed at the idea, put forth by "scientific management" consultants like Frederick Taylor, that diverse people could fit interchangeably into mechanized production systems like cogs in a machine. Instead, Scott suggested, effective management would evaluate people, evaluate jobs, and focus on making the right match between the two.

Edwin George "Ed" Booz, born in 1889, entered Northwestern as a freshman in 1908. During the next six years, he earned a bachelor's degree in economics and a master's in psychology; he also became Walter Dill Scott's protégé. Early photographs of Ed

THE WRANGLER
April 21, 1923

EDWIN GEORGE BOOZ

Were I giving a toast to the Wrangler of my choice on the occasion of the Twentieth Anniversary Banquet of my Fraternity, I would beg leave to propose the name of EDWIN GEORGE BOOZ, of the class of 1912.

"Ed" has been a friend of every Wrangler from the class of 1903 down to the class of 1926 in a personal way that has actually had cohesive power for the Chapter; as steward of the Active Chapter and as treasurer of the alumni organization for many years, he has contributed largely to the ownership of our present house and the sound financial basis we enjoy today; as a member of almost every committee of strategic importance since the founding of the Wranglers, he has contributed to his Fraternity that same gift of analysis and foresight that has enabled him to build up his own business organization in an entirely new field.

In "Ed" we have an example of at least one self-made man who has turned out a good product. Cast on his own resources at an early age, he "tied up" with the Wranglers for life. When "Ed" adopted us and we adopted "Ed," there was established a relationship that no mere court decree or passing of time could ever effect.

Here's to Ed Booz.

—DEAN LAKE TRAXLER.

In 1923 the Wranglers, Ed Booz's fraternity at Northwestern University, published a tribute, above, to him for its 20th-anniversary newsletter. Booz later was alumni treasurer and organizational advisor to the Wranglers, which in 1939 merged with Alpha Delta Phi. Right, students surround professor Walter Dill Scott in his Northwestern office.

Booz show a tall young man with a high forehead, a moustache, a strong jaw, owlish eyebrows, and a confident smile. He came across as determined, distinguished, and poised, despite (or perhaps because of) the fact that he continually had to work his way through school. His early jobs included waiting on tables, drafting, tutoring, bookkeeping, and conducting surveys and research in the industrial fields he was studying. People fascinated him, and his earnest but engaging manner made them fascinated in him as well. He had a cleft palate, which blurred his speech, but it was so well-integrated into his personality that, as his partner-to-be Jim Allen put it, "you didn't notice it after a while."

Booz's father was a timekeeper (he kept track of factory workers' hours) from Reading, Pennsylvania—a man of modest means descended from generations of glass blowers. Ed Booz himself, while an affable and convivial man, detested both drinking and smoking. When asked, "Mind if I smoke?" he would snap back, "Yes, I do mind!" Booz was stolid, Midwestern and square, somewhat unfashionable, full of gumption and earnestness. While at school, Booz worked at *Woman's World,* a magazine

based in Chicago, and at the Business Bourse, an early market-research firm, conducting analyses of sales and advertising. By the time he earned his master's in 1914, he had a set of marketable skills, a network of contacts, and the advice of two mentors—Walter Dill Scott and *Woman's World* advertising manager Thomas Balmer—that he should go into business for himself. He borrowed $500 from a local bank, State Bank and Trust Company of Evanston, in whose building he established his office. With a fraternity brother named Anderson Pace, he opened a small firm called the Business Research Service.

The Roots of Consulting

Ed Booz had an entrepreneurial frame of mind and he tailored his work to his clients' particular needs. His first assignments fulfilled the demands of the fledgling industrial era: finding competent executives (recruitment), office space (land surveys), and customers (market research). But his métier was in-depth consulting, what he called "taking the measure" of a business problem. He had a flair, as author Jim Bowman wrote in the 1984 book, *Booz•Allen & Hamilton: Seventy Years of Client Service,* "for probing and tinkering with American businesses, looking for soft underbellies or festering sores, nosing around companies whose leaders had a problem but weren't always sure what it was." His recommendations frequently included replacing or reassigning key people.

In 1917 Booz was drafted into the Army.

His mentor, Walter Dill Scott, oversaw the Army's personnel system, and Booz went to work for him, rising rapidly from private to major. He returned to civilian life in 1919, just in time for another recession but a short-lived one; it gave way to America's first 20th-century business boom, ripe for the talent of a man like Ed Booz.

In those days business people played golf and joked comfortably with each other, but when it came to talking about business problems they were reserved and close-mouthed, particularly in the face of new antitrust laws. In a competitive and bustling city like Chicago, conversation with a man like Ed Booz represented one of the few ways a corporate leader could step back and gain some perspective on the turbulent issues of his business.

Booz's reputation blossomed, buttressed by his predilection for publishing articles about business practice, often based on survey results. He produced surveys for the *Minneapolis Journal* newspaper and several Illinois banks. He conducted market research for the Illinois State Railroad (his first major client, back in 1914, seeking to know how customers might react to a rate increase); Addressograph, a then-famous maker of form-printing machines; Goodyear Tire; and W. F. McLaughlin and Company (purveyors of coffee since 1852). He surveyed

Ed Booz, left, was a major in the U.S. Army during World War I. Right, an early advertising card for the coffee purveyor W. F. McLaughlin and Company, one of Booz's early clients. Below, one of the first invoices of Booz's company shows separate line items for the services provided, the materials needed, and (presumably) travel and telephone expenses.

McLaughlin's
XXXX COFFEE

Greetings of different Nations, one of a series of twelve.   Esquim

1 Pound Coffee makes 30 Cups.
1 Doz. Eggs average cost 12 Cts.

It costs to settle a pound of Coffee as follows:

A FAMILY USING AT A MEAL

2 Cups Coffee,			15 Cents a pound.
4 " "			7½ "
6 " "			5 "
8 " "			3¾ "
10 " "			3 "
12 " "			2½ "

The glazing on McLaughlin's XXXX Coffee does the settling the same as eggs, and saves you the cost of eggs as shown above. The glazing is made of Corn Starch and Reclarified Sugar, therefore perfectly healthful.

W. F. McLAUGHLIN & CO.,
CHICAGO.

This card is one of a series of twelve, showing how the different Nations greet each other.

Sept. 30, 1916

Bureau of Railway Publicity,
1349 First National Bank Bldg.,
Chicago, Ill.

To Service $216.34

To Materials 10.30
        (Mailing Lists)

Miscellaneous Expense 11.50

                    Total --   238.14

locations for the Chicago Mercantile Exchange, Walgreen Drug Stores, and the clothiers Hart Schaffner and Marx.

The First Three Compatriots

Consummate in his care for clients, Ed Booz had a problem congenital to entrepreneurs: a carelessness about the evolution of his own firm. He took on a string of associates, but none lasted longer than a year or two until 1925. Perhaps for that reason the firm never had more than 30 clients in a single year during its first 15 years. Gradually, however, Booz attracted partners with the requisite skill to build a sustainable enterprise—and by 1936 there were three new partners.

The first was George Fry—a square-jawed, dark-haired young man as devoted as Booz to his business clients—who joined in 1925. Fry was instrumental in founding the New York office in 1935. He would stay with the firm through 1942.

Then there was James Lane "Jim" Allen, a dapper and handsome Northwestern economics major who made an unusually powerful impression on people, even at a young age. A few years after joining the firm in 1929 at age 25, he casually used the phrase "management consultant" in a Booz Allen brochure to describe his work. Although generally soft-spoken, Allen was strong-willed and strong-minded, unafraid to assert himself. When Ed Booz harshly critiqued one of his reports, Allen walked out for a day, snapping, "If you know so damn much about it, then you write it yourself!" He later recalled, "Of course, I came back the

next day and rewrote the report. It was much improved as a result of his pertinent comments."

Allen walked out again—for two years—in 1934 on the grounds that "we were not really running a business. We were individual practitioners." He returned in 1936 on the condition that he would become the administrative partner, responsible for the growth and development of the firm. From then until 1970, except for another one-year hiatus, he was captain of the enterprise. The firm grew under Allen's guidance and according to his tough-minded, pragmatic, and worldly view of life. To both Booz and Allen, a job was not successful merely because a client paid, or even when

a client was pleased. The client had to actually put Booz Allen's advice into practice. Allen was a visionary. He saw the long-term need to invest in a base, both for developing the capabilities of his people and for marketing the firm's name. This fueled a transition from boutique agency to mature partnership.

Carl Hamilton, who looked a bit like Woodrow Wilson, came to the firm in 1935 when he was 47 years old. He had worked previously at Weyerhaeuser, where he had managed a portfolio of service businesses. A specialist in marketing, Hamilton rapidly became a rainmaker for new business at

A 1923 Christmas Card from Ed Booz promoted friendship and business. Above, the four partners—Fry, Booz, Hamilton, and Allen, left to right—golfed together. Right, the partners and professional staff in December 1936. Seated, left to right, Hamilton, Booz, Fry, and Allen; behind them, Jim Olson (on couch arm), Dick Paget (standing), Mark Cresap, and four unidentified men.

SEASONS' GREETINGS

When you know we're with you,
and we know you're with us we both look forward with
more confidence and strength for the future.
We're sending this little appreciation of what
your co-operation means to us,
and what we hope ours may mean to you

EDWIN G. BOOZ SERVICE
BUSINESS SURVEYS

EDWIN G. BOOZ   ELMER D. BUSH

"...conversation with a man like Ed Booz represented one of the few ways a corporate leader could step back for a few minutes and gain some perspective on the turbulent issues of his business."

By Jim Allen

There used to be a firm in Chicago called Hibbard-Spencer-Bartlett. They were wholesalers of hardware—in those days, an important business. I spent one summer traveling with 40 of their salesmen, to see what they were doing with merchants were busy with their customers, setting up merchandise displays and writing ads. We found that the Hibbard-Spencer salesmen had nothing to suggest to these merchants, other than to lay down a 4,000-page catalogue

> [**"We found out that the salesmen were spending most of their time with their weakest outlets. There they had more time to talk about fishing, baseball, and the kids."**]

their time. We were trying to find out how they could make their services more effective through the independent hardware stores. Ward's and Sears were beginning to make themselves felt, and Hibbard-Spencer was trying to meet this new competition.

We found out that the salesmen were spending most of their time with their weakest outlets. There they had more time to talk about fishing, baseball, and the kids. At the busiest outlets, they didn't have any time to talk; those

and say, "Is there anything you want?"

On the basis of these findings, we helped them restructure their sales coverage. The outlets where volume was moving should get most of the attention. Hibbard-Spencer had to be of real service to these merchants, rather than just take orders. Out of this work grew the voluntary chain idea, the idea of chain brands like True Value Hardware, where the supplier would provide marketing techniques along with the merchandise.

Jim Allen, a Booz Allen founder and former chairman, told this story in a 1982 oral-history interview.

Booz Allen. Quiet and beloved by the others, he was known as the "flywheel of the group," in part because of the way he would race at the last minute to catch the 20th Century Limited train from New York to Chicago (it left at 4:30 p.m. and he never left the office earlier than 4:15). Hamilton wrote Booz Allen's first code of ethics, which among other things specified that the firm should never "take an arbitrary position about anything." In Hamilton's first year the firm began doing business as Booz, Fry, Allen and Hamilton.

"The Problem Is You"

Ed Booz built his business by cultivating people he called the "marines." These were key outsiders who could help a consultant gain the "first foothold ashore" with a potential client by speaking highly of the firm and its work. Today we might call this "networking." A marine, as one partner put it, was the kind of person you could call in the middle of the night without pre-arrangement. Most partners considered themselves lucky to have a list of 20 marines; Jim Allen, known for his gregariousness, had maybe 100. Then there was Harry Knight, an unusually well-connected partner with a list of as many as 400 terrific contacts—or so he said. Other partners called it his "owl list" because they'd call one of Harry's best marines, mention Harry's name, and the other person would say, "Who?"

The first major Booz marine was Sewell Avery, a board member of the State Bank and Trust Company of Evanston in 1919.

Avery became CEO of U.S. Gypsum, a cement company that was Ed Booz's largest client in the 1920s. Booz had helped Gypsum create what today would be called a "performance culture." There were too many "motors," he told one group of managers, and not enough "dynamos"—too many people consuming the spirit and power of the enterprise rather than generating improvement and new business. The motors, Booz said, should review their "assets and liabilities" and put themselves into a program of self-development, lest their managers do it for them.

In 1931 financier J. P. Morgan installed Avery as the CEO of Montgomery Ward, then the nation's number-two retailer after Sears, Roebuck and Company. Over the previous ten years, the nation's middle class had begun to coalesce and an ever-wider swath of America was united in the desire for a higher caliber of material goods. A market thus developed for the emerging industries that mass-produced clothing, furniture, housewares, tools, appliances, books, and toys. Ward had captured rural customers with its mail-order catalogs, but its leaders had made a near-fatal mistake. They had ignored the advice of one of their own executives, Robert Wood, who had proposed opening retail stores to tap the market of factory and office workers in newly expanding cities. Wood went to Sears, and his idea was so successful that he became CEO there; in 1931 Sears earned $9 million while Ward lost $8.7 million and faced bankruptcy.

Avery, coming in with a mandate for turnaround, called Ed Booz. Montgomery Ward

MONTGOMERY WARD & CO. RETAIL STORE — CENTRAL AVE. — ST. PETERSBURG, FLA.   6A-253

Montgomery Ward, above, brought high-quality inexpensive goods to many Americans for the first time. Ward's became Booz Allen's largest client in the 1930s. Consulting for firms like Walgreen's, Booz Allen helped lay the groundwork for new retail environments like this modern 1930s drugstore, left.

rapidly became his highest-profile client, especially after he helped design a first wave of reorganization and cost cutting that reversed Ward's decline. The retailer never caught up to its rival Sears, but by 1934 it was making money, and by 1936 profits reached $13.5 million annually. As Ward expanded to the East Coast, Booz, Fry, Allen and Hamilton opened a New York office to serve it. Back in Chicago, Ed Booz occupied an office at Montgomery Ward's Chicago headquarters, down the hall from Avery, who sent a car to pick him up every morning at eight. Booz became, as writer Jim Bowman notes, "Ward's top planning, organization, and personnel man." This latter role often meant mollifying senior managers antagonized by Avery, a brilliant executive whose surly personality had the effect of driving many senior executives from the company.

Sometime in the late 1930s Avery asked Booz to determine why so many managers were leaving. "The problem is you," Booz told him. This was true, but nobody had ever said as much to Avery and survived at Ward. This would be no exception; Avery abruptly ended Montgomery Ward's contract with Booz Allen. On the surface, this was a disaster. Booz never devoted himself to one client in that way again. But to Jim Allen, the post-Ward transition was a crucial springboard, "the nest egg around which many assignments of importance developed." Departing Ward executives had moved to the Marshall Field department-store chain, RCA, and the Chicago Title and Trust Company. They were solid "marines." They knew that Booz not only had helped save their old company from death, but that he had done one of the most difficult and trust-inspiring things a consultant could do. He had leveled with the boss.

A Basket of Blueberries

The late 1930s and early '40s were rela-tively easy for Ed Booz, who turned 50 in 1939. He took on a role mentoring younger partners, frequently lecturing them with advice such as, "Don't forget that human emotions are facts, and when you turn in your report I want those facts." Whenever an employee made partner—a decision Booz made on his own—Booz presented him with a basket of blueberries, hand-picked from the bushes on his Michigan country home. He wrote down aphorisms about life and work, which became known around the office as "Boozisms." He said people had six responsibilities in life: first to God; then to your family, including your extended fam-ily; then to your nation, community, and pro-fession; and finally to your organization or firm. Booz could be overbearing at times, but he was also a living model of his own advice. He did calisthenics every evening, he scheduled his times of relaxation and vaca-tion as episodes of self-improvement, and he showed up for every meeting on time.

"When he sat and talked to you," retired partner Bill Pocock said years later, "he got you under his skin." Booz reminded Pocock of his father and grandfather, both of whom had been ministers. Arnold Emch, another partner, recalled Booz correcting a report for the U.S. State Department in which Emch

Shortly before his death in 1951, Ed Booz penned this list of key attrib-utes for a high-quality individual. They became known as "Boozisms."

Start with character, intelligence and industry

Always spend less than you make

Daily - Think Right, Act Right, Eat Right, Sleep Right
Work Right, and Play Right.
Know your own Blind Spots.

Always willing to listen to and help worthy young men.

Require character, intelligence and industry
as the starting foundation in selecting personnel.
Pick the cream of men for your partners

To multiply, lend and divide with others.

Build a good list of substantial marines

Fear not the future nor people

"In all thy ways acknowledge Him and he shall direct thy ways".

The Name Game

BOOZ · ALLEN & HAMILTON

BOOZ·ALLEN & HAMILTON

Booz | Allen | Hamilton

Ever since its founding by Ed Booz in 1914, Booz Allen has done business under a succession of names. Here's a history of name changes leading up to today's Booz Allen Hamilton. The logo at upper left, Ed Booz's original "lighthouse" icon, was reclaimed in 1986 as the symbol for the Professional Excellence Awards.

1914: The Business Research Service

1916: The Business Research and Development Co.

1919: Edwin G. Booz, Business Engineering Service

1921: Edwin G. Booz Service, Business Surveys

1924: Edwin G. Booz Surveys

1935: Edwin G. Booz and Fry Surveys

1936: Booz, Fry, Allen and Hamilton

1943: Booz, Allen & Hamilton

1970: Booz·Allen & Hamilton

2001: Booz Allen Hamilton

evaluated the caliber of two dozen top people. Emch had used expressions such as "perhaps" and "quite possibly" throughout his evaluations. Booz crossed them all out. Emch protested: He wasn't *that* sure, and he didn't want to be unfair.

"Arnold," Booz replied, "we are hired to guide the superior executives to make a decision. As soon as you put in these qualifying words, you're putting doubt into the minds of executives, and hence we aren't really serving our purpose." He told Emch to rethink his evaluations until he felt certain and to rewrite the report accordingly.

It helped to have a leader who balanced backbone and spiritual presence. The work was intensive and the hours long. By the late 1930s an associate might have 15 or 16 projects going simultaneously. Travel was difficult and expensive; a consultant on a far-flung assignment (more than 1,500 miles from Chicago) would be allowed to return home only every third weekend. While on the road, he would interview people from top to bottom in a business along with the client's customers, scout locations for future work, and seek new recruits. He typically shared a hotel room with another consultant because—with consultants typically held in contempt as "efficiency experts"—budgets were tight. The value of management expertise had not been fully established yet.

Even when they were home, Booz Allen people routinely worked weekends and holidays. Jim Allen liked to tell the story of working on a report with Carl Hamilton one Christmas Eve. He took a break to buy his wife, Gertrude, a last-minute Christmas

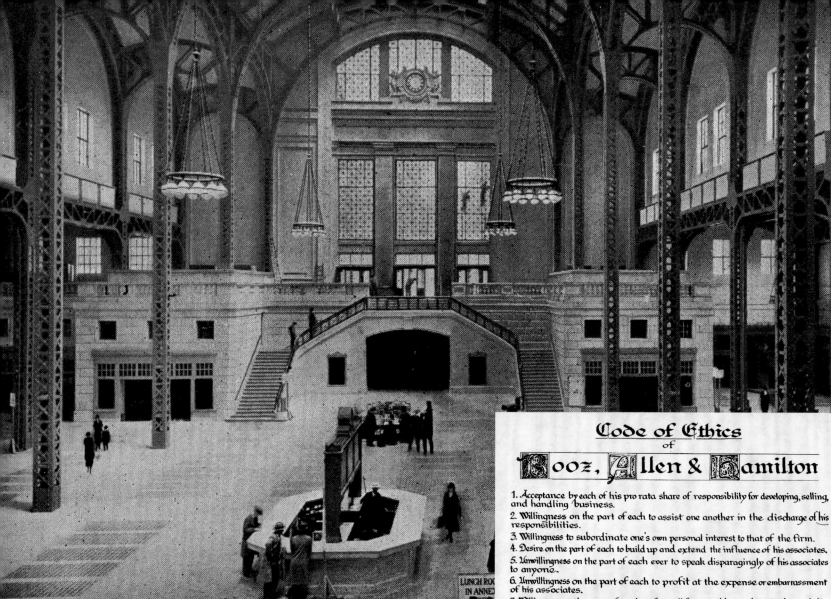

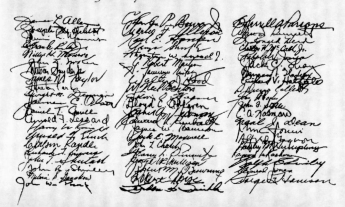

Code of Ethics
of
Booz, Allen & Hamilton

1. Acceptance by each of his pro rata share of responsibility for developing, selling, and handling business.
2. Willingness on the part of each to assist one another in the discharge of his responsibilities.
3. Willingness to subordinate one's own personal interest to that of the firm.
4. Desire on the part of each to build up and extend the influence of his associates.
5. Unwillingness on the part of each ever to speak disparagingly of his associates to anyone.
6. Unwillingness on the part of each to profit at the expense or embarrassment of his associates.
7. Willingness on the part of each to face all firm problems objectively and dispassionately without arbitrary or prejudicial position.
8. Willingness to offer constructive suggestion rather than employing destructive criticism.
9. Willingness to either sell one's ideas or to accede to the judgment of his associates.
10. Willingness to conduct one's personal life so as to reflect creditably both upon himself and the firm.

As an officer of Booz, Allen & Hamilton, I accept and approve this Code of Ethics to guide my actions.

present—a nightgown. Hamilton asked Allen to do him a favor: "Get my wife the same thing." Jim got to Marshall Field's two minutes before closing time. He said to the sales girl, "I want one of these nightgowns in size 8 and another in size 14," and he had them both gift-wrapped. When the sales girl handed him the gifts, she said, "I hope they never meet."

This code of ethics, written by Carl Hamilton in the 1930s, was periodically reprinted. Partners signed this version in the mid-1960s. Above, Chicago's Union Station, jump-off point for Hamilton and other rail-traveling Booz Allen consultants.

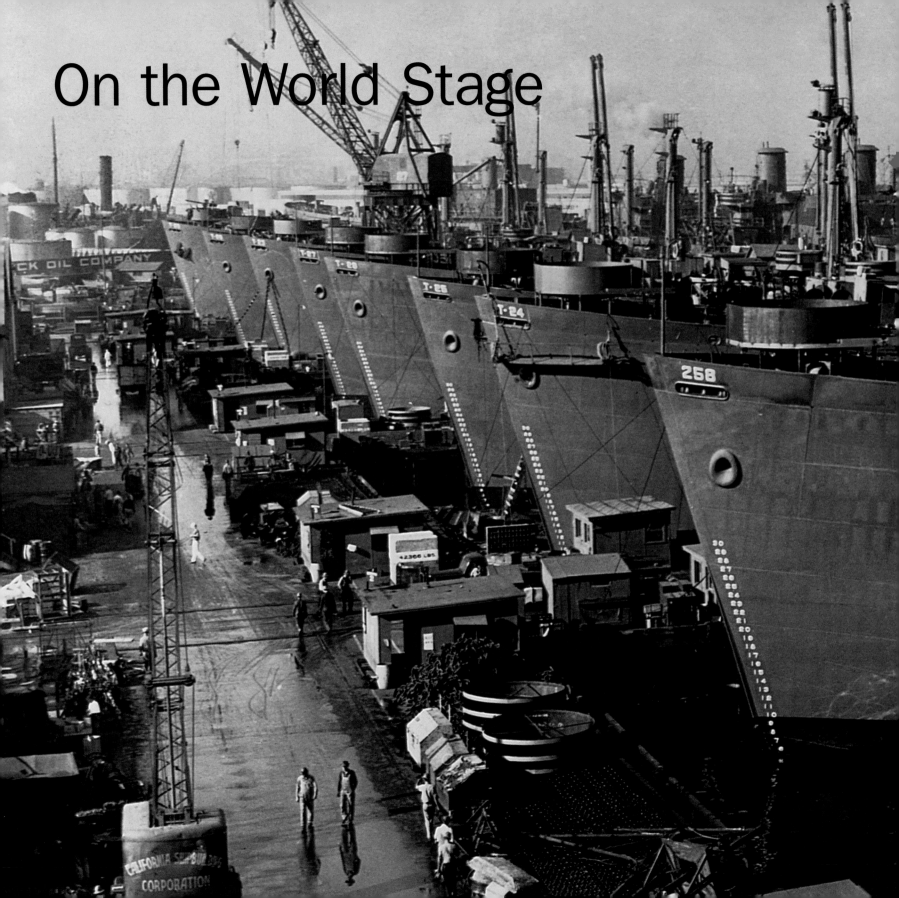

On the World Stage

World War II was a catalytic moment, particularly for the United States—an enormous leap in mobilization, distribution, management, and social science. Before the war began, with the country paralyzed by a crippling depression, it took the United States 200 days to create a warship. Within just ten months that was cut to 24 days, and by 1944 it was down to a week. The same miracle was applied to tanks, trucks, and bombs, and then, after the war, to cars, refrigerators, and radios.

For Booz Allen, the war was pivotal in a new, more expansive role as a partner to government. It launched the public-sector consulting business that is now a mainstay of the firm. It coalesced the firm's expertise in managing complexity, communications, and technology. It led to the loss of one partner, George Fry, and the welcoming of many more. It opened the door to classified work in military intelligence, cryptography, aerospace technology, and other burgeoning fields. Furthermore, it introduced Booz Allen to its longest steady client, the United States Navy.

Frank Knox contacted Ed Booz in 1940. A former member of Teddy Roosevelt's Rough Riders, Knox had been publisher of the *Chicago Daily News*, for which Booz had conducted organizational and salary studies, and in 1936 he was the Republican vice presidential candidate. U.S. President Franklin Delano Roosevelt, in a move to garner bipartisan support for a war effort while running for an unprecedented third term as president, had just appointed Knox secretary of the Navy.

By mid-1940 the tensions of war had rarely seemed so dire. The Axis powers controlled Czechoslovakia, Poland, Norway, Belgium, the Netherlands, and France. England seemed certain to fall next. Imperial Japan had landed troops in Saigon and—unbeknownst to many—Germany, Italy, and Japan had signed a pact pledging that if any one of them declared war on the United States, the others would also.

Knox had written a series of magazine articles promoting the idea of a two-ocean navy, one that could simultaneously win campaigns in both the Atlantic and Pacific. A week after Knox took office, Congress made his vision policy, but the Navy was grievously under-equipped to deliver on it. It had a force of only 190,000 and just 385 combat-ready ships. Its headquarters were in a temporary building left over from World War I, and its telephone, internal mail, and intelligence systems were far out of date.

"Men, what's our job?" Knox asked his admirals. "To double the Navy," they replied,

estimating that it would take about four years. "We have only half that time," Knox said. "It must be done by 1942."

Ed Booz and Jim Allen took on the assignment personally. Allen inspected shipyards up and down the East Coast. Their first recommendation: permanent headquarters. This idea went up the chain of command to FDR, who agreed: "I don't want any more temporary buildings in this war." Booz Allen suggested ways to revamp the Navy's systems and services, cutting red tape, replacing old chains of command with new management units under each Navy bureau, and structuring ways for them to work together. Then Booz Allen's people moved in to implement the recommendations. A 28-year-old partner named Richard Paget was inducted into the Navy as a lieutenant and placed in charge of a new office called "Management Engineer." He and his wife shared a modest Washington apartment with Ed Booz.

Placing a consulting firm within the established bureaucracy had a catalytic effect on streamlining the system. Each Navy bureau had its own Booz man—Arnold Emch in Medicine and Surgery, Perry Addleman in Ships, and Paget in the secretary's office. "If I had a personnel thing to handle," Emch recalled, "I wouldn't go through the formal channels. That would take three weeks. I would just call up my Booz counterpart in the Bureau of Personnel and it was done by tomorrow morning. We never told the admirals how we did it. They looked upon us like miracle workers."

Left, U.S. Navy Rear Admiral Clark Woodward starts the machine that drives the first rivet in the keel of the 45,000-ton battleship *Missouri* at the Brooklyn Navy Yard, January 6, 1941. Even with the Navy Yard at the busiest time in its history, the warship wasn't scheduled for completion until three years later, in February 1944. Above, at his desk in the 1940s is Secretary of the Navy Frank Knox, who masterminded the rapid acceleration of Navy production and hired Booz Allen to help make it happen.

The Andrews Sisters entertained troops and sold war bonds with their music, while posters rallied Americans back home to the Allied effort in World War II. On the lines, a military nurse cared for a wounded soldier. Far right, a destroyer (the smaller ship alone in the rear, at right) shepherded freighters across the Atlantic in a convoy during the prolonged Battle of the Atlantic, in which American, British, and Canadian naval forces broke the dominance of German submarines. By this time, Booz Allen Hamilton was involved with every branch of the U.S. military.

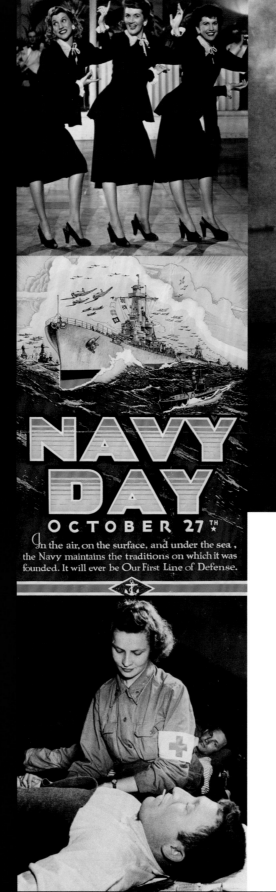

Never Spent Money "More Effectively"

Early in 1941 the U.S. Army asked Booz Allen to help rethink its structure as it had done for the Navy. The consultants delivered their report to Army Secretary Robert Patterson on December 6, 1941. The next day the Japanese bombed Pearl Harbor and, as writer Jim Bowman put it in Booz Allen's 70th-anniversary history book, "these exercises in organization went from war preparation to war footing."

Besides drawing the United States into the war, the attack had shifted the balance of military sea power. The Japanese had destroyed 12 U.S. battleships—most of the Pacific fleet—forcing the Navy to exploit remaining strengths in submarines and aircraft carriers, whose power ultimately was superior to the enemy's. This rapid strategic shift, combined with the urgency of fighting a two-front war, made both military branches receptive to change. When officers balked at working with the Booz Allen consultants, the consultants were promoted to higher ranks;

at age 31, Paget became the youngest captain in Navy history.

Within four years the Navy had become the most powerful in the world, with 3 million people, 9 new battleships, 19 first-line aircraft carriers, more than 500 destroyers and escort ships, more than 100 submarines, and thousands of amphibious ships and other craft. Booz Allen also helped the Army, Veteran's Administration, and Navy jointly agree on medical terminology, promising injured soldiers better care and compensation than ever before, especially as their

cases crossed jurisdictional boundaries.

Speaking of Booz Allen's role in the war effort, Knox was quoted by *Fortune* magazine in 1944 as saying that he had never spent the government's money "more effectively." The firm's work earned it an enduring place in the U.S. military's future in both war- and peacetime. Since World War II the United States has been the world's most technologically and organizationally advanced military power, and Booz Allen has remained a trusted advisor and resource for technological support to all branches of the defense department.

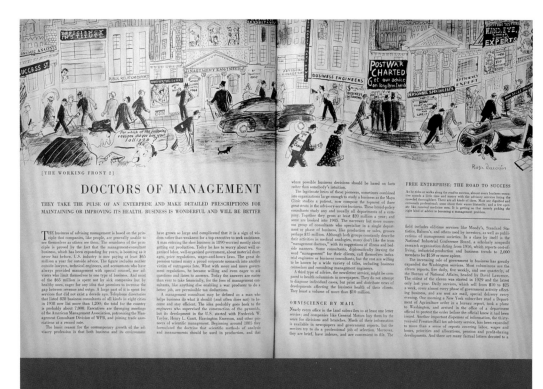

In July 1944, *Fortune* magazine published what was perhaps the first general article about management consulting. It surveyed the field, cited the first professional society for management consultants (the Association for Consulting Management Engineers, or ACME), which Edwin Booz and Jim Allen had helped found and in which they remained active, and looked ahead at the bright future of the field.

"Management consulting is so new," reported *Fortune*, "that the question of nomenclature and aims has given the association, which includes a number of strong individualists, many stormy sessions. Three professional writers failed at the task" of explaining what the ACME stood for. But the necessity of professional standards was clear: U.S. industry spent $65 million a year for outside advice, "a large part of it for services that did not exist a decade ago."

Of the seven management consultants profiled with pictures in the article, Edwin G. Booz was first. *Fortune* briefly described work Booz Allen Hamilton had conducted for the U.S. Navy and Montgomery Ward: "One of the many reasons why Ward was losing money, [Booz] discovered, was that its retail stores were run by men with only mail-order experience. Some management advisers will tell you that [Ward CEO Sewell] Avery now should take some good labor-relations advice."

Buying the Oriental Rug

George Fry didn't think much of government work in the early 1940s. Maybe it was lucrative at the moment, but he believed the future was with business. Rival firm McKinsey & Company was rising fast, carving out a niche as advisor to corporate CEOs and board members. Booz Allen already enjoyed such a role and it could compete solidly with McKinsey—but not, in Fry's mind, if Booz and Allen spent all their time doing war work in Washington. When were they coming back to Chicago?

Ed Booz felt there could be no more important work than military consulting—at least until the war was won—but he also didn't see any inherent contradiction between commercial and government work. Hamilton and Allen were caught in the middle. In 1942 Hamilton had a heart attack. Although he kept a full workload, saying, "I refuse to be an invalid," he took himself out of the debate. Now as "the buffer between Ed and George in the line of fire," Allen felt stuck, and he left the company. He took a job at Hall Brothers, publishers of Hallmark cards, hoping his departure would force Booz and Fry to resolve their disagreement. It did. Fry left, selling his partnership interest and taking several clients and associates with him. (Fry's new firm, first called Fry Lawson & Co. and later Fry Consultants, would be acquired in 1967 by ARA Services, forerunner to today's Aramark.)

Allen came back to Booz Allen in 1943, returning, as he had in 1934, with a condition—that the firm create a formal process to make decisions. He formed an executive committee with neither Booz nor Hamilton on it. Allen was chair; John Burns, a new partner, took on administrative responsibilities; the third member was Harold Smiddy, a brilliant consultant who drove himself and everyone around him furiously, as he slept only five hours per night. Coincident with the changes, the firm adopted the name Booz, Allen & Hamilton.

Suddenly it was as if some hidden barrier had been lifted. In 1945 the number of partners leaped to eight, overseeing a roster of 129 associates and support staff. There was more than enough business to support them. Government contractors that Booz had advised during the war, such as Sperry and Olin, were growing into highly successful commercial enterprises; they still needed Booz Allen's help and perspective. Offices opened in Los Angeles in 1945, Minneapolis in 1948, and Washington, D.C., in 1949. So many new consultants were hired that they were housed five or six to a bullpen-like room, each with his own desk and file drawer. They traveled so much they were never sure they'd have the same desk when they came back.

The growth was disorienting to Carl Hamilton. Struggling with ill health in 1946, he watched the firm move to larger headquarters on the 17th story of the Field Building in Chicago. On the floor was a beautiful, expensive, oriental rug—symbol of the trappings of stability: salaries, a formal bookkeeping

A Booz Allen Hamilton company card circa 1946, left, and the firm's partners in the early 1940s, above. Seated, left to right: Jim Allen, Ed Booz, and Carl Hamilton; standing, Edward J. Burnell, James C. Olson, Harold F. Smiddy, John L. Burns.

department, a reception area. "All our problems started," Hamilton was heard to say, "when we bought that goddamn oriental rug."

Ed Booz, too, was wistful for the days when he presided over a tiny firm. At one meeting he said, as if realizing for the first time the ramifications of growth, "Our expenses last year were a million dollars. Imagine our little firm spending a million dollars." For his desk, he brought in a round dining-room table from home—the same table around which he and his partners had hashed out business problems late at night during the early years. He returned from a Hawaiian vacation with a box of chocolates, stopping at every desk to give one to each employee.

"He was trying to keep it his little firm," former Vice President John Gallagher recalled, "and it just wasn't in the cards." Booz no longer decided who was going to be a partner (that decision by then was made by a small group of senior people), but he insisted on presenting the news himself, still in the form of a basket of blueberries.

Call the Prospect and Tell Him the Truth

When an aerodynamics engineer named Harry Vincent joined Booz Allen in 1949, the personnel manager took him around to meet Jim Allen. "Don't forget," said the manager, "his name is Jim. And your name is Harry." Allen shook his hand and said, "I welcome you warmly to the firm. I hope you'll have a wonderful time here, and don't ever hesitate to come and see me whenever you want."

Bespectacled, tall, and elegant, Allen was shy at times yet gregarious and gracious. He often came across as austere. "Mr. Allen's office in Chicago was sort of sacred ground," remembers retired Senior Vice President Paul Anderson. "You didn't go in there unless you had permission. And you had to go through the palace guard of administrative staff." Jim Allen was the primary decision maker. No one made partner until Allen, who had a veto in the selection of partners, saw him or her on an assignment.

Allen had a talent for cultivating friendship and a rare gift for seeing patterns across time. In May 1949 he published one of the first articles on human capital— "A Company's Most Valuable Asset," for *Central Manufacturing District Magazine*. Senior corporate executives were on average seven years older than their counterparts had been a decade before, Allen observed. Looking ahead, the pace of executive retirement would take many companies by surprise, and (he wrote) they had no pipeline of people being groomed as replacements. News of the article was carried in *Time* magazine, the *Wall Street Journal*, *New York Herald Tribune*, and other influential media.

Allen and Booz shared the trait of outspoken honesty. When now-retired Senior Vice President John Shutack, then a new partner, wrote a proposal for a job he secretly felt wasn't worth taking on, Allen homed right in on his ambivalence. Calling Shutack into his office, he asked, "John, do you really want to do this work?" When Shutack admitted

Jim Allen, in portrait at far left, joined the firm in 1929, coined the term "management consultant" a few years later, and went on to become chairman of Booz Allen from 1946 to 1970.

Above, these candid snapshots from the early 1950s show scenes from a picnic at the Connecticut home of partner John Burns and his wife, Beryl, soon after Burns moved his practice from Chicago to New York.

"At parties, Booz Allen partners and their wives put on skits and sang around the piano. Ed Booz taught the wives to do conga dances."

Ed Booz, Gertrude Allen, Jim Allen, Helen Booz

JAMES L. ALLEN
135 SOUTH LA SALLE STREET
CHICAGO, ILLINOIS

July 12, 1949

Dear Betsy and Bill,

Every one of us seemed to have such an enjoy-
able time in our "Off-Duty" moments at the May
gathering that we thought you would like to have a
pictorial record of the occasion.

Until our next get-together, as Stewart Lowry
would say.

Aloha,

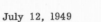

mag

Mr. and Mrs. John W. Pocock
2501 Thayer Street
Evanston, Illinois

Parsons	Humphrey	Bowen
Burnell - dec.	Eldridge	Morris
Allen	Kubert	Coulter
Booz - dec.	Lowry - dec.	Wise
Olson	Addleman	Browning
Burns	Knight	Pocock
Campbell - dec.	Porter	Hanson
Emch		

Partners' dinners, like this one, left, from May 1949, were full of revelry. Clockwise from foreground: Hope Bowen, Bill Pocock, Arnold Emch, Minna Emch, Ruth Campbell, Charlie Bowen, Betsy Pocock. Pocock and Bowen had recently joined the firm. Allen's characteristic graciousness is evident in his follow-up note. Above, the two founding partners and their wives: left to right, Ed Booz, Gertrude Allen, Jim Allen, and Helen Booz.

that he didn't, Allen said, "It really shows!" and made the younger partner call the prospect and tell him the truth.

Partners in the early 1950s tended to be in their 20s and 30s, married (often with young children), hardworking, responsible, and close to one another. Their wives, who almost universally didn't work outside the home, socialized together. At parties they put on skits and sang around the piano. Ed Booz taught the wives to do conga dances. Partners who undermined or undercut each other, or who were seen as abrasive at their colleagues's expense, were frozen out. Training for consultants consisted of an hour learning about policies from the office manager and the rest of the day writing digests of old reports, some of which had been written by Booz in 1915 or 1916. Seniority didn't matter; retired Senior Vice President Harry Vincent, then a new consultant, came in one day and found out that one of the most senior people in the office had been fired. "Well," he said to himself, "if I was looking for high opportunity and high risk, I just found it."

As full of optimism as the late 1940s and early 1950s were, there were two sad moments. Carl Hamilton had his second, this time fatal, heart attack in 1946. Ed Booz called everyone into the library to tell them personally. Booz himself died in 1951 after suffering a stroke. By that time there were some 25 partners. Judging from the things they said and wrote years afterward, they were keenly conscious of the legacy of values that Ed Booz had left and eager to put them into action.

Three Hundred People and $7 Million in Revenue

In the surge of American postwar growth, Booz Allen's consulting work involved the kinds of technical and philosophic shifts that enabled mid-sized regional companies to quickly grow to national, or even global, scale. Often this involved structuring changes or new ways of thinking about markets; generally, the starting point was when a president or CEO recognized that there must be a more effective way to operate than the company's present capabilities or idea set allowed.

In the early 1950s there were essentially two competing consulting firms—Booz Allen Hamilton and McKinsey & Company—and each had enough business to guarantee its growth. Booz Allen and McKinsey consultants all knew how to move in the highest levels of business and society. They knew how to present cogent analyses, pulling together knowledge, experience, and perspective into well-written, sophisticated-looking reports with short- and long-term recommendations, and cost-benefit analyses of factors that might affect success.

The major difference between the firms was in culture. McKinsey was glamorous, MBA-centric, and oriented toward offering advice. Consistent with Jim Allen's brief but explicit statement of values—"The best way to sell business is to do good work for our clients"—Booz Allen people were doers, pragmatists who considered no engagement a success unless the client acted on the recommendations and got results.

Carl Hamilton, in portrait at far left, joined the firm in 1935. A rainmaker for new business, he also wrote Booz Allen's first code of ethics. Booz Allen partners, left, held a retreat at the Shawnee on the Delaware resort, owned by musician Fred Waring, in 1951. Left to right, Bill Pocock, Perry Addleman, John Burns, and Lloyd Wilkinson.

Clients in the early 1950s included John Deere, the farm-equipment manufacturer, which increased sales from $490 million a year into the billions by decentralizing operations and making every factory responsible for its own design, testing, and manufacturing; and Allstate, which with Booz Allen's help expanded from writing only auto policies into a full-service insurer. Booz Allen helped Kraft Foods implement the first computer system used by a consumer-products company to analyze the way food was distributed to wholesalers and retailers, worked with United Airlines to help parlay in-flight passenger comfort and convenience into a source of competitive advantage, and dispelled Cessna's illusion that there were 300,000 potential customers who could afford private planes (the number was closer to 60,000). Other clients were Anderson Clayton, Parker Pen, Pet Milk, Pillsbury, RCA Victor, IBM, Studebaker, Hughes Aircraft, NBC, a number of newspapers—and *Playboy* Magazine,

which entered the client roster surreptitiously under its parent-company name, HRH Enterprises. When Jim Allen found out, he shook with anger. Booz Allen's reputation was not to be compromised that way.

Booz Allen preserved its reputation through other means as well. Its consultants, all men at the time, wore dark suits, white shirts, and hats when outdoors. Hair was short. Cigars were (mostly) forbidden. As a "Booz man," you were expected to be well-groomed and poised enough to enter a boardroom and hold your own. Your wife was expected to abet your career—tolerating your travel, hosting social gatherings, and, according to a 1955 corporate policy, making an "overall contribution to the esprit de corps, harmony … and general welfare of the corporation." Finally, you were expected to engage in the social and civic life of the community. Jim Allen provided a living example of this, maintaining, for example, a lifelong relationship as a fund-raiser and guiding

PERT: Nailing Complexity to the Wall

The first project-management technology began as a sketch on a tablecloth in the lower grill room of the Hay Adams Hotel in Washington late in 1957. The U.S. Navy's Special Projects Office (SPO) had asked Booz Allen and Lockheed to help organize the Polaris nuclear submarine project so that the missiles it fired would be ready when the submarine launched. It was one of the most tightly scheduled projects ever undertaken by the Navy in peacetime. The deadline depended on meshing dozens of simultaneous, interdependent activities.

U.S. Navy Captain John A. Dudley presents Bill Pocock with a Polaris flag to commemorate the PERT program in 1957.

Over lunch Booz Allen partner Bill Pocock and Gordon Perhson, SPO's deputy director for administration, tried some metaphors: a hydraulic system of flows and outputs, a network of electrical charges, a simple mathematical model. Gradually they settled on a critical-path framework—a time-line-style diagram showing all the different activities in parallel, with the "critical path," featuring the most important interdependencies and bottlenecks, highlighted in thick lines. Suddenly, there was a cry of horror behind them. It was the waitress, looking down at the linen tablecloth, scribbled full of flow diagrams, decision trees, and equations. Perhson added $20 to the tip, folded up the tablecloth, and handed it to Pocock. Eight weeks later, they had their method codified—they named it Program Evaluation and Review Technique, or PERT—and the Polaris was under way.

By the 1960s PERT was nearly ubiquitous. Every complex project in government or industry had some kind of critical-path chart plotting its sequence and workflow, specifying prerequisites, estimated costs, and accountabilities. PERT led to project-management software, first on mainframes in the 1960s and ultimately on personal computers. Some Booz Allen consultants got their start as PERT virtuosos. But as retired Senior Vice President Paul Anderson notes, the real value of a PERT chart came from influencing behavior: "Every time I posted the flow chart on the wall, I'd draw a red line through the critical parts. People would come into the office, look at the chart, and say, 'My name's on that red line! What do I have to do to get off it?' And they'd meet their deadlines."

Booz Allen never patented PERT and undoubtedly missed some royalties as a result, but its reputation as PERT's inventor has generated business for the firm ever since.

New Uses and
Management Implications
of PERT

BOOZ·ALLEN APPLIED RESEARCH Inc.
Scientific and Technical Services

"The best way to sell business is to do good work for our clients"

spirit to Northwestern University's J. L. Kellogg School of Management.

Blind Spots and the Product Life Cycle

Herbert Fisk Johnson Jr., better known as "Hib," was the third-generation CEO of S. C. Johnson Company, maker of varnishes, paints, polishes, and stains derived from carnauba wax, which was produced from the leaves of the Brazilian wax palm. The privately held company based in Racine, Wisconsin, had a longstanding relationship with Booz Allen. Jim Allen sat on the Johnson board, as Ed Booz had before him. The company was a pioneer in consumer marketing and employee satisfaction; it provided paid vacations in 1917 and a pension plan in 1934. Hib was a successful and beloved CEO, but he had two blind spots. If he hadn't overcome them, one of Booz Allen's first big contributions to management thought might never have come to light.

One of Hib's blind spots concerned his son Samuel, a Harvard graduate being groomed as his father's successor. One day in the early 1950s Jim Allen walked in on a vigorous argument between them. Hib had placed Sam's desk in a corner of his own office. "That's the best way to teach him

how to run the business," Hib explained. "He can see what I do." Allen suggested an alternative tactic—giving Sam a chance to make a name for himself in a separate department that he could direct on his own. At Booz Allen's suggestion, Sam ended up running a new-products department—which coincidentally was set up to address Hib's other blind spot: his veto of every new-product proposal not based on carnauba. Other executives could see it was time to diversify, but Hib stubbornly had refused to see beyond the product line that had made his company successful.

At the time, many companies considered product development a risky gamble. Often executives couldn't agree on which products to support, technical breakthroughs came to market but customers didn't buy them, and products floated for years inside corporate laboratories, eating up development costs. Undaunted, Sam dove into his new job with enthusiasm. He spent nights discussing product development with his friend Conrad Jones, a junior member of the Booz Allen team. Jones was a bit of a polymath, with a keen interest in evolutionary theory and a notion that it could be applied to business.

One night, Jones went to a blackboard and sketched out a curved trend line, one that climbed up in a steep hill and leveled

off in a plateau, to illustrate "what happens to products over time." All products, he proposed, followed the same pattern, from birth to (usually) gradual growth to maturation to decline. No company could rely on a single offering; only a suite of products, with new ones always in the pipeline and a systematic process for bringing them to market, could stave off competitors. The theory was counterintuitive because its two main metrics—sales volume and profit margins—rose and fell at different rates. But it appeared accurate enough to effectively guide decision making.

Sam bought in, and with Hib's blessing the company revamped its approach to product development. Beginning in 1955 S. C. Johnson introduced a series of aerosols, including Glade air fresheners, Raid insecticides, Off insect repellents, and other new products—all wildly successful. Sam Johnson and Conrad Jones co-authored the article "How to Organize for New Products," published in the May-June 1957 issue of the *Harvard Business Review* (HBR). It became HBR's best-selling reprint for the next 20 years. Although the article is often credited with introducing the product life-cycle concept, neither Jones's diagram nor the term "product life cycle" appeared in it. Instead, the article spelled out ways in

Wernher von Braun, shown here with a model of the German V-2 rocket, was instrumental in the development of the U.S. guided-missile program and, later, the first moon launch. An early Booz Allen assignment for the U.S. Air Force brought the firm together with von Braun and his former boss, Major General Walter Dornberger.

which companies could develop new products rapidly and consistently.

Years later Jones reminisced, "I was 31 years old and soon to know the ultimate in professional bliss: my creation spreading around the world like wildfire, adopted as state-of-the-art and becoming standard practice, with experts everywhere pontificating on my very words…" Sam Johnson, meanwhile, went on to run S. C. Johnson's international operations and became president of the company in 1966. He died in 2004.

Booz Allen and the Cold War

"We've got some problems with our guided missiles," said Major General Frederick M. "Hoppy" Hopkins, head of the U.S. Air Force's Industrial Mobilization Division. "We don't know anything about missiles," replied Booz Allen consultant Bill Pocock, who later served as president of Booz Allen's public-sector consulting business. The general locked the door to the office where they were talking. "Well," he said, "anybody would have to learn, and you folks can."

It was 1949, at Wright Air Force Base near Dayton, Ohio. Since the end of the war, Booz Allen had continued to work for the government, taking assignments for the Veteran's Administration, Civil Aeronautics Board, Army Corps of Engineers, and Air Force. But the missile-development project on Hopkins's mind was something different. On the surface, it was highly technical: consultants would be called on to audit, plan, recruit, and check the advances needed for an entirely new form of aeronautic technol-

ogy. The emerging challenge, however, was to help the government advance its technological competence in general to meet the new challenges of cold-war geopolitics. Over the next 50 years, intelligence and military services would have to learn how to adapt to new types of warfare (like guerilla war and terrorism), manage and respond to weapons of unprecedented scale and complexity, keep classified secrets safe in a world of global telephony and computers, maintain accountability to democratically elected officials, operate across new types of international partnerships such as NATO, and remain within the limits of government budgets. This was arguably the first time that Booz Allen had been called in to help the U.S. military develop those capabilities—but it would not be the last.

As of the late 1940s, guided missiles existed only as prototypes in research labs. Booz Allen consultants reviewed every missile-research project in existence and estimated what would be required in plant space, production staff, materials, and cost to produce them. They worked with experts from Nazi Germany's V-2 rocket program who had come to the United States after World War II. These scientists, including Wernher von Braun and Major General Walter Dornberger (von Braun's former boss), eventually became the core of the American missile program and, later, the first moon launch. But they were initially prisoners of war; at least a few of them lived in a quarantined section of Wright Air Force Base known as The Cage, where the Booz Allen team met with them. Dornberger spent some of

Booz Allen's Evolving Government-Consulting Structure

Booz Allen established an enduring position as a government consultant by serving the U.S. Navy during World War II, but Ed Booz had done market research for the Illinois State Railroad and other public-sector clients as early as 1914. Here's how Booz Allen has organized and delivered its public-sector work over time.

1940: The firm begins to serve the U.S. federal government with an engagement for the U.S. Navy.

1949: Booz Allen & Hamilton opens a Washington, D.C., office to serve primarily U.S. federal government clients. It evolves into the Government Services Group.

1955: The firm forms a subsidiary called Booz Allen Applied Research, Inc. (BAAR-INC) to meet cost-structure regulations for public-sector consulting, primarily for the military and technology branches of the U.S. government. Its offices are in Maryland—first Frederick, then Bethesda.

1964: During the early 1960s, another practice emerges: consulting for non-defense clients such as state and local governments, churches, hospitals, and higher education. Booz Allen's government business enjoys strong growth in the late 1960s.

1970s (early): As Booz Allen goes public and the defense consulting business declines, BAARINC shrinks dramatically.

1970s (mid): Government consulting begins growing again. Technology Management Group is formed.

1973: Two divisions handle government consulting: Booz Allen Applied Research and Government Services.

1979: A new Booz Allen Public Management & Technology Center (PMTC) is established.

1980s (early): The PMTC now includes four main divisions, respectively focused on management and information systems; defense acquisitions and logistics (including military training and NASA); communications, electronics, and information; and transportation consulting.

1980s (late): The PMTC gradually evolves into two new Technology Centers: Applied Sciences Center and Information Technology Center.

1991: The Technology Centers are renamed the Worldwide Technology Business (WTB), which focuses on consulting to the U.S. government. Booz Allen offices worldwide enter a new era of advising government agencies, particularly around privatization.

1992: Outgrowing its Bethesda workplace, WTB moves to a new building in McLean, Virginia, which eventually grows into a five-building campus.

1994: As an outgrowth of Vision 2000, WTB employs cross-functional project teams to provide strategic consulting and technology-implementation services to public-sector clients of all types.

Because they consulted to agencies whose work was classified, BAARINC consultants and staff were among the first at Booz Allen to wear corporate identification tags, like this one from the 1970s.

"Fear not the future nor people." — *Edwin Booz*

To those behind the Iron Curtain, the launch of Sputnik seemed to prove the superiority of the Communist system. Left, a Soviet poster celebrating Sputnik, and above, a model of a Sputnik-like satellite displayed at a Prague exhibition in 1957.

his time in custody at the Booz Allen office in Chicago. "We'd give him a box of cigars and a typewriter," Pocock later recalled. "He would type answers to our questions in German and then translate them into English."

Meanwhile, a newly created Booz Allen missile group analyzed reconnaissance photos of Soviet "birds." Then-consultant Harry Vincent identified the capabilities and characteristics of the missiles in the pictures, and estimated how many could be used in a conflict. Other analyses identified the Caspian Sea as the target range for Soviet test missiles, a fact the U.S.S.R. attempted to hide. Booz Allen compiled all the estimates of Soviet missile potential into a highly classified report with a red leather cover, known around the Pentagon as the Red Book. "The funniest thing happened," Pocock recalled. "About 12 years after we wrote the Red Book, I was down at the Pentagon. One of the colonels said, 'Do you suppose we could show our reference book to Pocock?' They brought it out 'for my eyes only' and I opened it up and said, 'Look, team.' There was my name on the author's page."

To coordinate the nation's fledgling missile program, Booz Allen recommended creating an Office of Guided Missiles at the top of the defense department. K. T. Keller, former president of Chrysler Motors, became its first director in 1950, but the missile initiative didn't gain much traction for the next seven years.

At about the same time, Booz Allen took an assignment developing an electronic intelligence strategy for the U.S. Air Force. The contract, which involved developing technology to monitor radar and other telecommunication signals, was for the biggest single job Booz Allen had been awarded to date, and it represented a dramatic new threshold for the firm. The Air Force had ruled out nontechnical organizations, particularly management consulting firms, as contractors, and the selection of Booz Allen was a welcome validation of the firm's technical competency. There was one problem, however: a wall had to be built between government consultants, who would work with classified information, and the rest of Booz Allen; otherwise the entire firm would have to go through the government's complex clearance process. As a solution, in 1955 the firm created a subsidiary called Booz Allen Applied Research, Inc. (popularly called BAARINC). For the position of chief scientist, it recruited George Shortley, a Princeton physicist and operations research expert who had co-authored the leading textbook on atomic spectra. Air Force leaders began referring to BAARINC as their "chosen instrument" for guided-missile research, and the unit rapidly outgrew its origin in a Bethesda, Maryland, garage.

At its zenith BAARINC generated about 40 percent of Booz Allen's revenues, but it steadily grew apart from the rest of the firm, culturally as well as operationally. As a result,

a fracture now existed between the firm's commercial and government consultants, one that became worse from time to time and would take well into the 1990s to heal.

The Triple Shock of Sputnik

On October 4, 1957, the Soviet news agency Tass announced that "the first artificial earth satellite has now been created [and] was successfully launched in the U.S.S.R." The Soviets called it Sputnik, "traveling companion" in Russian. Though just the size of a beach ball, able only to send a simple A-flat beep back to earth, and pooh-pooh'ed as a "bauble" by American politicians, Sputnik was a triple shock to the United States. First, losing the space race hurt America's pride—especially since the U.S. Navy and Army Air Corps had worked on Earth-orbiting-satellite proposals as early as 1945. Second, Sputnik seemed to demonstrate the U.S.S.R.'s technical sophistication, along with its ability to produce and foster young scientists. Third, the power and precision of the rocketry required to place Sputnik in orbit convinced many that the Soviets had the capacity to accurately target U.S. cities. Soviet Premier Nikita Khrushchev's antagonistic behavior toward the West exacerbated a fear that Americans were in more danger than previously thought. Whatever Khruschev's intentions, the launch of Sputnik, which circled Earth 1,400 times before burning up in the atmosphere, established a tone of one-upmanship in relations between the Soviet Union and the West that lasted for four decades.

Toronto newspaper readers learn of a U.S. missile failure a few months after the Soviet Union's successful launch of Sputnik—the first human-made satellite to orbit the Earth. This challenge to America triggered a set of responses in which Booz Allen Hamilton would play a significant role.

In 1949, the first cargo of Marshall Plan-financed Caribbean sugar shipped to war-torn England arrives, welcomed by British author Lytton Strachey, U.S. AID representative E.M. Holgreen, and (at far right), assistant agricultural attaché D. W. Kling. Booz Allen opened its international subsidiary in 1956 to help new industries sponsored by the Marshall Plan thrive.

Based on its experience in missile work, BAARINC found itself in the thick of the American response to Sputnik. The United States had been beaten in part because of inter-organizational rivalries and complacency. Now there was a new sense of urgency. Von Braun, by now a director with the Army Ballistic Missile Agency in Huntsville, Alabama, had been trying to get a spacecraft into orbit; he had the technology but not the budget. He called Booz Allen to ask for help justifying the budget, and the U.S. missile program was soon on a fast track.

U.S. President Dwight Eisenhower set a goal: to develop guided missiles for military and peaceful uses, as well as for manned space exploration. The Army team, led by von Braun, successfully launched the first U.S. satellite, Explorer I, in 1958. For manned space exploration, Congress created the National Aeronautics and Space Administration (NASA) that same year. BAARINC and its successor divisions at Booz Allen would be deeply involved with the space agency as organizational and technical consultants for the next 40 years. Over time the Office of Guided Missiles evolved into a general research office; ultimately, under the new name Defense Advanced Research Projects Agency (DARPA), it became most famous as the creator of the Internet, but it also made important contributions in sensing, surveillance, communication, and stealth technology.

The Sputnik launch may have given the Soviets a head start, but they were soon undone by their own reliance on the absolute power of the state, which controlled everything. Jobs as complex as missile or space programs can't be handled by government alone. In Western nations, by contrast, the cold war was forcing a merger of the previously separate domains of military research, civilian science, business R&D, and public and private education into autonomous but allied partners.

The First Steps Overseas

Booz Allen had first sought business outside the United States in 1952 when partner Ralph Smiley, after hearing a speech by U.S. President Harry Truman about the Marshall Plan, proposed to his fellow partners that they offer an international consulting service. "Inevitably," Smiley recalled, "we would be thrown into going abroad, and we'd better be prepared for it. I visualized that we would have offices around the world, just like those in New York and Chicago. The European offices would eventually be headed by Europeans, and the Japanese office by Japanese. We would keep all these people from splitting off through an exchange of people where we could give them better training and more advanced thinking in management and technical know-how."

Jim Allen supported the idea, but many partners wanted no part of it; they had all the business they could handle in the States, and the world outside seemed unfamiliar and threatening. As late as 1949, in fact, there had been a written Booz Allen policy against conducting work outside the

In the 1950s Booz Allen helped restructure the customs operations and textile industry in Egypt, and create a land-registration system in the Philippines. Above, cotton Egyptian hats. Left, the Philippines' Mount Bongao and the stilt houses of the Badjao people.

United States. "We weren't equipped for it," Allen explained later. "We didn't want to get into it until we could handle it." It seemed too difficult to find Europeans or Asians with the background to become Booz Allen consultants. Nor did the Americans make it easier. When foreign-born consultants came to Chicago or New York for training, they sometimes had to endure unenlightened remarks from the staff.

Nonetheless, Allen allowed Smiley to take on several overseas assignments beginning in 1953: a land-registration system in the Philippines, a restructuring of Egypt's customs operations and textile

industries, and work for Iran's national oil company. Consultations with Italian steel, oil, and chemical companies followed in 1956. To develop the work in line with the U.S. Agency for International Development (administrator of the Marshall Plan funds that were supporting the reconstruction of Europe), Booz Allen created a subsidiary, Booz Allen & Hamilton International Inc. (BAHINT). Booz Allen opened its first international office—in Zurich, a safe city in a neutral country and a central point from which to travel—in 1957. It would be three more decades, though, before non-U.S. partners played the kind of pivotal role at

Booz Allen that John Smiley had envisioned.

By 1958 most of the ad-hoc, seat-of-the-pants procedures of the firm's early years had been replaced. There were now 300 people in the firm, about 50 partners, $7 million in revenues, and offices in Chicago and New York, as well as in Cleveland, Dayton, Detroit, Frederick (Maryland), Los Angeles, Philadelphia, San Francisco, Seattle, Washington, and Zurich. All prospective employees would go through ten two-hour interviews with partners plus three days of intelligence, personality, and aptitude tests to ensure they could meet the challenges of the firm's increasingly diverse business.

The Go-Go Years

New Yorker writer John Brooks used the phrase "the Go-Go Years" to describe the full-speed-ahead bull market that energized Wall Street for most of the 1960s—a decade of dramatic growth and conglomeratization but ultimately collapse and retrenchment. The first part of the decade was a wonderful time to be a management consultant. Business boomed, and Booz Allen's share expanded.

Late in 1959 *Time* magazine featured Booz Allen as the "world's largest, most prestigious management consultant firm," crediting the PERT process for producing the Polaris missile two years ahead of schedule. A few months later *Business Week* put Jim Allen on its cover: "By definition and design," the article proclaimed, "[Booz Allen] is an extraordinary operation." It wasn't obvious from the article exactly what management consultants did, but Booz Allen was clearly at the top of the field.

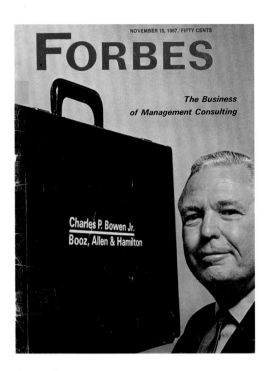

Charlie Bowen and his briefcase made the cover of *Forbes* magazine on November 15, 1967. The Booz Allen president was featured in a profile of the firm titled, "The Instant Executives." At that time, the article said, management consulting was growing at a rate roughly twice that of the economy. *Forbes* estimated Booz Allen to lead the profession with $37.5 million in annual billings. Right, television was a catalyst for a cultural change in people and their institutions.

In 1962 Booz Allen changed its legal status from that of a partnership to a corporation so it could offer better pension and profit-sharing options to its partners and staff. McKinsey had made the same move for the same reasons several years earlier. Under this new structure Jim Allen became chairman of the board; Allen then named partner Charles P. "Charlie" Bowen president. Bowen was the first Booz Allen president to base himself in New York rather than Chicago. A former aeronautical engineer, he was a feisty, outspoken man, a gifted storyteller, and something of an iconoclast. As early as the late 1940s he had refused to follow the Booz Allen dress code, saying, "I don't own any white shirts and I don't propose to buy any. I don't like them."

During Bowen's ten years as president, Booz Allen multiplied in complexity. It developed a larger, more intricate management committee; an increased international presence; and separate profit centers specializing in such disciplines as computer services, market research, and industrial engineering consultation. The client roster also began to change. Booz Allen traditionally had had a mix of large and small clients. Now consultants focused their attention on financially sophisticated blue-chips like Chrysler, Goodyear, R. J. Reynolds, Borden Foods, Nestlé, The Kellogg Company, and Citibank—which were show-

ing that companies that sought growth through acquisition and profit management could outperform those which tried to expand only by trying to introduce and sell more products.

Booz Allen found an increasing amount of business from brokerage firms and investment banks that had never before asked for consulting help. Jim Farley, then based in the New York office, was called in to help brokerage Eastman Dillon rework its operations; that led to work with several investment banks. They, too, were operating in a new world, learning how to deliver the new financial instruments their customers demanded.

It was easy in the early 1960s to step back and see how dramatically the world was changing. Media expert Marshall McLuhan proclaimed that people and their institutions would inevitably adopt the habits and culture displayed on television. Consultant/author Peter Drucker, a specialist in corporate and social-sector strategy, argued that government and corporate organizations would grow to resemble each other. Leadership consultant Warren Bennis and sociologist Philip Slater predicted that the Soviet Union would collapse. Within Booz Allen, Charlie Bowen foresaw that "multinational corporations will grow to the point where they have problems they don't understand yet, and neither do we, and we'd better be ready for them."

According to his view, consumerism in particular would have a strong impact, and customers would soon demand quality, safety, and reliability as they got used to a world of readily available goods. Bowen also foresaw the day when any management consultant who didn't use a computer would be obsolete. "We've got guys who are dragging their feet," he said, promising that "we won't compensate them [and] we won't promote them." Booz Allen's early embrace of computing as an inevitable way of life was one of the factors that kept the firm alive for the next two decades.

Going Places

The cut-loose atmosphere of the 1960s had its effects on Booz Allen as well as on nearly every other workplace. A Rat Pack cigar-and-martini culture pervaded the business world. The civil rights movement, the awakening of feminism, the Vietnam War and the protests against it, cultural shifts that started with popular music and moved into television, and the assassinations of John F. Kennedy, Martin Luther King, and Robert F. Kennedy all contributed to a backdrop of uncertainty, turbulence, and violence behind the smooth, upward-flowing curve of stock prices. No one knew at the time how these waves might break; many corporate leaders dismissed them at the time as all but irrelevant. Yet in 1968, from the Booz Allen offices on K Street in Washington, D.C., one could see smoke rising from fires set a few blocks away in riots following

The 1960s were a period of hope, dreams won and shattered, and a shifting of values in culture, the arts, and business. In the United States, the civil rights movement transformed the status of African Americans, while the nation was shocked by the assassinations of Martin Luther King Jr., President John F. Kennedy, and U.S. Senator Robert F. Kennedy. The Volkswagen bus was an icon of hippie culture, the Beatles led the British domination of 1960s rock and roll, and the conflict in Vietnam escalated with the July 1964 attack on a U.S. destroyer in the Gulf of Tonkin.

reflections

By John Wing

An assignment for the Coast Guard sent our team around the U.S., looking at their maintenance of buoys and maritime navigation structures. On one trip to Alaska in a little seaplane, my client—a Coast Guard captain—sat next to me. All of a sudden, the door next to him flew open. I grabbed

> ["I yelled up to the pilot, 'Hey, the door's open here!'"]

onto my client and yelled up to the pilot, "Hey, the door's open here!"

"No problem," he called back. "It happens all the time. There's a rope in the overhead. Get it and tie up that handle." We did. It worked. I'll always remember that as the time we saved not just the project, but the client.

Retired Senior Vice President John Wing led Booz Allen's Transportation Consulting Division. He told this story in a 2004 interview for this book.

Martin Luther King's assassination. Retired Senior Vice President Ed Hearle remembers trying to decide whether to evacuate the building and wondering, if people did, where on earth they would go.

Booz Allen had always had a strong transportation portfolio in its commercial and government practices, starting with the Illinois railroads back in 1914. In the 1960s computer modelers began to analyze the complexities of transportation. The affluence, technological advances, cosmopolitan mood, and changing demographics of the 1960s "baby boom" led to an across-the-board jump in pleasure travel, commuting—and congestion. Planners at the Bureau of Public Roads, forerunner to the National Highway Administration, wanted help forecasting the most effective places to invest highway money. The National Highway Traffic Safety Administration, newly created in the 1960s, asked for Booz Allen's help evaluating facilities for repairing and testing new safety devices. One project ultimately birthed antilock brakes. The Norwegian Caribbean Lines wanted to cut costs, so a team of Booz Allen consultants had the onerous assignment of spending two months on cruise ships in the Caribbean, assessing operations.

Booz Allen also helped the U.S. Maritime Administration rework shipping routes and financial structures to reinvigorate ocean trade. It evaluated container-ship designs that used catamaran-shaped hulls to skim over the water on a cushion of air. The concepts were not commercially viable, but the Navy applied similar technology to its amphibious fleet.

Wall Street was energized by a bull market for most of the 1960s, a period in which business adopted sophisticated financial practices and made increasing use of new financial instruments, such as options and other derivatives. Booz Allen helped many leading corporations, investment firms, and brokerage houses in a flurry of mergers, acquisitions, and other changes geared for a go-go business environment. The trading floor of the New York Stock Exchange, seen in this overhead shot, was often the nerve center.

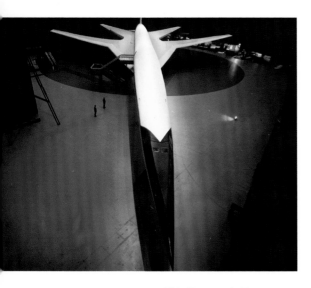

This Supersonic Transport (SST) aircraft, shown in a full-size mockup at the Boeing Developmental Center in Seattle, Washington, would have flown at 1,800 miles per hour. Unfortunately, as a Booz Allen study in the 1960s showed, it also would have been economically and environmentally unsustainable. Right, the moon sets over the Earth in a shot taken from the Space Shuttle Discovery in 1995. Booz Allen has been a consultant to NASA since its creation in 1958.

Perhaps the most significant transportation work conducted by Booz Allen in the 1960s involved recommendations *not* to proceed. In the mid-1950s European governments had prototyped supersonic transport (SST) planes, adapting military technology in hopes of replacing ordinary jets for long-distance travel. During the Kennedy administration, the U.S. Department of Transportation (DOT) asked four outside groups, including Booz Allen, to evaluate whether the United States should heavily subsidize SST research and development. The Booz Allen team concluded that SSTs would never be financially competitive; they also foresaw damage to the Earth's ozone layer and public opposition to the noise of sonic booms. The DOT, whose top officials supported the SST, challenged the Booz Allen report, but the firm held to its findings. SST transport never got off the ground in the United States, even after two more attempts in the Nixon administration.

In 1966, consulting for NASA, Booz Allen predicted that the Orbiting Astronomical Observatory would last little more than a month. NASA rejected the study and launched the satellite anyway; it failed after a day in orbit. Since then new observatory satellites have been launched with ever-increasing life spans, thanks in part to subsequent Booz Allen technical recommendations. The firm contributed to the design of the Hubble Space Telescope, launched in 1990, which was planned for a 15-year operational lifespan. Booz Allen also was involved in the theoretical strategy for the 1969 Apollo 11 moon launch, which put the

first humans on the moon. Working with two other consulting firms, Booz Allen recommended that the command module Columbia with its lunar lander attached should enter Earth's orbit first, then fire out of the planet's atmosphere toward the moon before heading toward the moon's surface.

Going Long

There are very few people who, when the grandchildren ask, "What did you do at work?" can say, "Well, let me tell you about the NFL." Former Booz Allen Chairman and CEO Jim Farley is one of them.

In 1966 Farley took a phone call during his lunch hour. It was Jim Kensel, right-hand man to Commissioner Pete Rozelle of the United States' National Football League (NFL). Farley met with Kensel and then with Rozelle that afternoon; the next day, Rozelle engaged Booz Allen to assist with the merger of the National and American Football Leagues. The motivation was television. During the previous few years, the audience for professional football had exploded; the NFL sold rights to its league games for $4.6 million in 1961 and tripled that to more than $12 million in 1964. The American Football League (AFL), which had formed in 1959—almost 40 years after the NFL—positioned itself from the start as a television-friendly network, with long pass plays and reverses, colorful uniforms, and team logos. When competition for television money intensified, the rivalry between the two leagues became acrimonious. In 1966 the leagues, which had previously agreed to honor each others'

Booz Allen recommended that the command module Columbia
with its lunar lander attached should enter Earth's orbit first,
then fire out of the planet's atmosphere toward the moon before
heading toward the moon's surface.

contracts, began to steal each others' players.

Rozelle believed a merged NFL-AFL could stem the inter-league rivalry, but there were enormous complications: some cities had two teams; federal antitrust laws would need to be waived; each team was its own independent franchise, raising serious business concerns; and Rozelle himself often clashed with the AFL commissioner, Oakland Raiders' owner Al Davis. Nevertheless, Farley thought this the most challenging and romantic assignment imaginable. He visited every club, owner, and manager in both leagues. He recalls walking on Hawaii's Waikiki Beach with Vince Lombardi, the 235-pound coach and CEO of the Green Bay Packers, who reached over and bumped Farley's shoulder to make a point. Farley, conscious of his slender build, said, "Vin, one more of those and I'm out of here."

With Booz Allen's help, the merger overcame every hurdle. Congress exempted the new league from antitrust laws on October 21, 1966. The new National Football League debuted that fall, and the following year ABC's Monday Night Football paid $8 million to televise just one game a week. Another result of the assignment: in his conversations with Farley, the Brooklyn-born Lombardi let slip that he would love to return to the East Coast. A few weeks later, the owner of the Washington Redskins told Farley his team was looking for a new coach. "Well," said Farley, "I do know someone looking ..." Three weeks later, news of Lombardi's move to the Redskins appeared in the *Washington Post*.

The Green Bay Packers defeated the Kansas City Chiefs, 35-10, on January 27, 1967, in Super Bowl I—the first national championship game played following the merger of the American Football League and National Football League in the United States. Above, NFL Commissioner Pete Rozelle celebrates the union on October 1, 1966, holding together two footballs labeled with the acronyms of the old leagues.

Even during the fiercest war years in Vietnam, the Vietnamese people and American expatriates (such as those working for Booz Allen) struggled to preserve everyday life. Here are two shopping scenes in the central market of Saigon; right, a visitor selects fruit in 1964; above, just before the Tet holiday (roughly equivalent in Vietnam to a combined Christmas and New Year's) in 1970.

Going to Vietnam

As harmony prevailed over the new football league, half a world away a proxy war between the world's two superpowers was worsening. Against this backdrop, around 1966, BAARINC, Booz Allen's government consulting arm, evaluated the communications equipment used by South Vietnamese and American soldiers. They trained South Vietnamese soldiers, designed highways and electronic fences, and in a series of projects named after ducks (TEAL, MALLARD) they revamped defense communications systems, ultimately engineering a switch from analog to digital technology.

This was BAARINC's first military field experience, and it set a precedent for consultants visiting the theaters of combat. Some consultants went to Saigon for so long that they brought their wives.

Bill Pocock's wife, Betsy, remembers staying at a hotel on the Saigon River and visiting the homes of Booz Allen staff members and their wives. In what must have been a surreal existence, they coped with the stress of living in a war zone by emulating life back home—playing tennis and bridge amidst encounters with military police and funeral processions.

Back in the United States, in 1967 Booz Allen took part in key strategic decisions—most memorably the closing of the defense department's Springfield Armory in Massachusetts. Cyrus Vance, then deputy defense secretary, called Harry Knight, who referred the call to Harry Vincent, then head of the Booz Allen Washington, D.C., office.

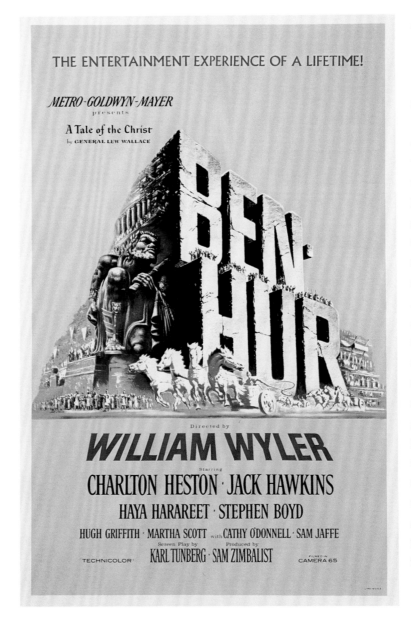

A Booz Allen engagement in the 1950s helped spark a well-known shift in Hollywood. At the time, major studios kept large in-house staffs of stars, directors, and producers, financed by profits from the theater chains they owned. But in the late 1940s, antitrust lawsuits forced them to divest the theaters; then, with the rise of television, ticket sales dropped. Jim Taylor (later president of the firm) led a Booz Allen team that advised Metro-Goldwyn-Mayer to reduce costs by shifting its film-making to independent producers. *Ben Hur*, released in 1959, was one of the first MGM films made under the new system. It won 11 Academy Awards and generated enough profit to convince the industry of the new approach's viability.

The desire for industrial
development led the
Algerian government to hire
Booz Allen in the 1960s.
This scene is from a rolling
steel mill in the Algerian
city of El Hadjar.

Vincent met on a Saturday morning with Vance and Defense Secretary Robert McNamara. McNamara boasted that he had ordered 600 bases closed and he hadn't made a mistake yet. But the Springfield Armory was the government's oldest munitions manufacturing site, set up by George Washington in 1794, and the Congressional delegation from the Bay State was howling in protest. McNamara was steadfast; it cost too much to keep open.

Some of Booz Allen's most senior executives took on the assignment. They interviewed dozens of people and found that there was in fact no financial rationale for the closure. But McNamara told the Booz Allen team, "You made a mistake. You never interviewed me." It turned out that he had used cost as an excuse when the reality was that Springfield was not equipped for the new, innovative weapons R&D that the military needed. "In our final report, we told the truth," Vincent recalls. "Yes, the U.S. had a basis for closing the armory—not costs, but their capacity for innovation."

Going International

By the middle of the 1960s even the most recalcitrant people at Booz Allen recognized the importance of being an international firm. But how? Should they buy overseas firms and risk taking on consultants who might never meet Booz Allen's standards? Should they choose a few target locations and develop business step by step but risk missing out on other opportunities or investing heavily in unprofitable locations? Or should they simply expand to meet assignments that came their way and risk losing out to strategically minded global firms?

Booz Allen tried all three approaches. In the end, Edwin Booz's original dictum turned out to be the best guide: building a successful international practice depended, first and foremost, on recruiting teams of quality people in the arenas where the firm wanted to operate. Booz Allen helped build oil fields in Iran and then worked to revitalize the Algerian wine industry. Booz Allen consultants created strategic studies for mining and steel industries in Brazil and Venezuela, with much of the work supported by the World Bank. Work with the Latin American banking sector led to a permanent office in São Paolo in 1969; a study for the Mexican Tourist Bureau led to the development of Cancún as a vacation spot. In Europe, Booz Allen opened an office in London to establish a presence there, and in Düsseldorf to replace the Zurich office, which the firm closed because of the limited availability of Swiss work permits for foreigners.

Where possible, Booz Allen established these international offices around managers and consultants native to the locale; Senior Vice President Gerd Wittkemper, for example, was among the core consultants who joined Booz Allen in Düsseldorf. In other cases, a few young Booz Allen partners from the United States tested themselves (and the firm) by managing overseas offices. Cyrus Freidheim Jr. brought his family to Brazil; John Rhodes Sr., new to the firm after a career in the international oil business, actively recruited consultants in Europe.

Chuck Allison, then in his early 30s, arrived to take over the London office without ever having been in the United Kingdom. A prospective client, the managing director of Colman's Mustard, soon arrived for an exploratory meeting. When it ended, Allison didn't quite know how to address his guest. So he looked at the gentleman's business card and said, formally, "Thank you for coming, Sir Richard Colman Bart." He only later learned that "Bart" was an abbreviation for "baronet."

Going Public

Two memorable events occurred at a partner's meeting in Puerto Rico late in 1968. A group of young partners threw Charlie Bowen into a swimming pool with his tuxedo on, and Jim Allen announced within the firm that Booz Allen was going public. Five hundred thousand shares of its stock would be offered on the New York Stock Exchange in January 1970 at $24 per share.

Most start-ups reach a moment when the founders retire and need to cash out. There are typically three ways to raise the money: set it aside in advance, borrow it, or sell the company to the public. The third route, if you can manage it, is often cause for celebration in the moment—and in the case of Booz Allen, partners cheered; most held only a few shares, but if the firm's fortunes continued to grow they would make a fortune in the future. They didn't begrudge Jim Allen or other senior partners their millions; they had, after all, built the firm to its current enviable position. "The old guys get their due," Freidheim later remembered saying to himself, "and now it's our firm to take over and run."

Moreover, going public would allow the firm to use its stock to expand through acquisition. There was only one problem, although it wasn't yet apparent in Puerto Rico. Within a year after the stock offering in early 1970, the management consulting business shifted for the worse. The Go-Go years were over. The economy plunged into recession; corporations stopped thinking about growth and so needed less help managing expansion. Government work also suddenly dried up in the aftermath of the Vietnam War and the winding down of U.S. President Lyndon Johnson's Great Society programs. Even seemingly solid contracts, like the MALLARD battle-communications initiative, lost their congressional sponsorship and evaporated.

The downturn affected the entire profession, but Booz Allen suffered worst. New competition from Boston Consulting Group and Bain & Company appeared. Older partners retired, vaporizing key personal relationships with client executives. Within Booz Allen the emphasis on share prices distracted people from the cornerstone principle of helping clients succeed. "We turned into a collection of urgent salesmen," one partner recalls. Jim Allen and Charlie Bowen

From 1970 to 1976, Booz Allen's stock, whose certificate is shown below, was offered on New York's over-the-counter (OTC) exchange, the forerunner to the National Association of Securities Dealers Automated Quotations (NASDAQ) exchange.

retired but remained on the firm's executive board, Bowen as chairman. James W. "Jim" Taylor, head of the New York office, became president in 1970.

Taylor was popular and well-respected, and he took the mentoring of others seriously. He could be fast-talking, sharp-tongued, and quick to lash out but also graceful in taking it back. He took criticism easily and laughed at himself unpretentiously. Now-retired Senior Vice President Harry Vincent once complained, "I'm tired of you kicking me in the shins every time I talk to you." Taylor replied, "If I got you in the shins, it's only because I missed." Unfortunately, Taylor hitched the firm's star to the go-go strategy of growth through acquisition. Booz Allen acquired eight smaller firms between 1970 and 1974. These included a chemical-testing lab, an airport-design firm, a product-design company, and the first market researcher for cable television. Partners left client work to run them. The company positioned itself as a "supermarket of services." In the social-Darwinian atmosphere of the era, it seemed appropriate to let them compete against each other.

"It was well-intentioned, but it turned out to be very disruptive," recalls Daniel Idzik, a now-retired senior vice president who had just become the firm's general counsel. It also kept overhead high, even as billings dropped in the early 1970s. The firm coped at first by closing offices. Retired Chairman and CEO William Stasior, then a senior consultant to the public sector, remembers being the "last one to turn out the lights" in

Booz Allen Applied Research's Chicago office. Booz Allen's stock price dropped below six dollars a share by 1972.

That same year the firm's leadership asked three young partners—Dick Reagan, Paul Anderson, and Al Meitz—to study the firm's administrative capabilities. They got permission to analyze Booz Allen's prospects as they might for a client, and what they found was sobering: if nothing changed, the most valued partners would leave. The young partners presented the report to the five most senior executives: Jim Allen, Jim Taylor, Jim Farley, Jim Newman, and Charlie Bowen. Anderson recalls that when they finished "there was dead silence in the room. Just nothing, for what seemed like an eternity. Finally, Mr. Allen cleared his throat and said, 'I think these are interesting findings. We need to give them serious consideration.' That was interpreted by everybody to mean Allen blessed the work."

Anderson remembers thinking to himself, "This is what management consulting is all about." If Booz Allen couldn't take the tough medicine of meeting business realities, how could it advise anyone else to do so? The Reagan-Anderson-Meitz report, which came to be known in Booz Allen as the RAM report, was one of several factors leading the firm's senior management to recognize the need for a shift of direction. In January 1973 Booz Allen President Jim Taylor resigned. The firm named Jim Farley, who had formerly run the Cleveland office, as Bowen's successor as president and as CEO soon afterward.

reflections

By Bill Stasior

In the early 1960s, I was able to attend Northwestern because of a scholarship program for caddies started by the famous amateur golfer Chick Evans. Years later, after I became CEO of Booz Allen, I visited Jim Allen in Florida and learned that he had been one of the founding contributors of the Evans Scholar Program.

[**"Without Jim Allen's generosity, I probably wouldn't have gone to college."**]

I was struck by what a small world this is, by how the past affects the present and future, and I realized that, without Jim Allen's generosity, I probably wouldn't have gone to college—at least not a college of Northwestern's caliber. And I most probably would not have joined the firm.

When he heard this story, Jim commented: "Well, the investment has obviously paid off."

Bill Stasior, Booz Allen Chairman and CEO from 1991 through 1999, told this personal story for a commemorative booklet published after the death of Jim Allen.

Turnaround

J im Farley was as surprised as anybody when he was named Booz Allen's president in 1973. "I never thought I was really in the race," Farley said. Farley was 43 years old, and his relative youth symbolized the firm's new direction. Jim Allen and his colleagues, in their 70s, had retired, and many other executives in their 50s and early 60s had left. Only four partners from the government side of the business remained where once there had been 16.

At Farley's inaugural meeting as president, Chairman Charlie Bowen handed him a sealed envelope. "Open this in private," he said. "It's everything you need to know to run the company." Farley, standing in front of everyone, immediately tore it open. Inside was a blank sheet of paper. The symbol-  ism was clear: no one knew quite how to save Booz Allen from its troubles, but they would rebuild the com- pany from scratch together.

As president, and later chairman and CEO, James Farley led Booz Allen through its turnaround period of 1973 to 1984. Farley sparked the firm's "fire in the belly" by taking the firm private, revitalizing its spirit, and overseeing the resuscitation of its commercial and government practices in tandem with an improved business climate.

Farley was a gifted administrator and, like his predecessors, he had a steel backbone. He had run the Cleveland office, had consulted primarily to financial services companies, and at the time he was chosen to lead Booz Allen he successfully had been managing the computer systems department—even though he didn't have a technology background. He was affable, quick to smile and put his arm around people, and not very formal. He was also a private man who rarely talked about his personal life or his feelings, even to people who worked closely with him for years. His colleagues learned to translate his malapropisms (such as "absotively!") and his coded "Farleyisms." When he said, "Explain that again to me?" it meant that he didn't accept the answer and wanted another one. His blasé "How we doing?" was an invitation to interest him.

Farley's first move showed both his sincerity and willingness to overcome rivalry. He approached Harry Vincent, who had just moved from head of the government practice to executive vice president and who had been another candidate for the president's slot, and asked him to help design the firm's comeback. "For the following year," recalls Dan Idzik, then-general counsel, "Jim and Harry were almost inseparable." Farley and Vincent appointed a cabinet of senior officials—the two of them plus the heads of the major business units (Jack Lesher, John Rhodes Sr., Conrad Jones, and Bill Sommers at first) and the top three administrative officers (Ed Schwallie, Paul Anderson, and Dan Idzik). They never had worked as a team before, but now met once a month in no-holds-barred sessions aimed at turning the firm around.

The cabinet brought out Farley's natural gift for convening people to common purpose. Once, after being handed a thick, dense proposal on business development, the members started bickering over the details. Farley stopped them and told them to meet after dinner—"and one cocktail only, fellas." That evening he sat them in a circle. "I've read the proposal," he said. "One third makes a hell of a lot of sense. One third is absolute garbage. And one third I'm not sure about. We're not leaving this room until we find out which is which."

"The business grew because we were highly incentivized. We had meetings every Monday morning in New York, where we would ask each other: 'What are you going to sell this week?' If you didn't sell, we would not eat."

The Long March Back

Farley pushed relentlessly for taking the firm private. He felt it a necessary step to inject "the fire in the belly," as he put it—to kindle a partnership spirit and "make our guys feel like winners." Farley and Lesher, who would later become Booz Allen's president under Farley, talked with some of their Wall Street clients about a leveraged buyout (LBO). Using debt to take over a company, particularly from the inside, was a relatively new idea, and few people knew how to put together such a deal. Ironically, the firm's sunken value made an LBO plausible; once business improved, the share price would likely rise and the purchase price would go up, making it more difficult to finance. They would have to act quickly.

To forestall legal challenges or the appearance of impropriety, the firm hired Salomon Brothers and Goldman Sachs to evaluate the deal; it could only go through if both firms agreed on the price. They settled on $7.75 per share in what became the largest-ever LBO involving a consulting firm. Continental Bank, then the firm's long-term bank, and Japan's Daichi Kangyo put up the funds, about $10 million. Idzik and CFO Ed Schwallie played crucial roles in securing the money. "I remember Ed Schwallie being on the phone when we were leaving Chicago for a meeting in New York," Idzik recalled at a 1999 meeting of former Booz Allen employees. "We were about $1.5 million short and he spoke to Continental Bank, and we got on that plane and we didn't know if we were going to get [it]. We got to New York and

they gave us the $1.5 million."

The banks accepted the partners' guarantees of future earnings as their only collateral—an enormous vote of confidence because if the firm didn't thrive, the banks had no way to collect. Idzik, meanwhile, devised a plan in which Booz Allen would loan partners money to buy shares at a discount—ensuring they wouldn't gain the full value unless the partners stayed for ten years. This practice remains in place today, encouraging partners to cast their lot with Booz Allen for the long term.

Following the return of the firm to private ownership in 1976, what remained, of course, were the details of rebuilding the firm. By the 1980s Booz Allen's senior partners had reinvented the firm's governance structure as well as its culture. They relocated the headquarters from Chicago to New York's Park Avenue. They intensified the recruiting of graduates from Harvard, Stanford, Wharton, and Northwestern while actively seeking a more ethnically and gender-diverse workforce. They managed Booz Allen more collegially and democratically. They placed a new emphasis on quality and ethics. They expanded the firm's presence in Washington, D.C., and Europe, and sold many of the businesses Booz Allen had only recently acquired.

Fortunes soon turned, thanks to the new energy in the firm and an improved business climate. The commercial consulting business recovered, lucrative international opportunities developed, and the government-consulting business began to pick up.

In the public sector, for example, the

reflections
By Ed Hearle

In the early 1980s, on an assignment for the United States Conference of Roman Catholic Bishops, we were asked to suggest ways of organizing Catholic Relief Services to run more effectively. We reached a point where, being 75 percent sure of our recommendations, I wanted to check them in

[**"I knew I had impressed him but I didn't know why."**]

advance with senior people within the church. I asked for a meeting with Terence Cardinal Cooke, Archbishop of New York City.

As you might expect, he was a formidable individual, but he didn't express it through pomp, a raised desk, or an imposing office. He was simply dressed and he met me in a sparse anteroom, with just a couple of chairs and a table. I was deeply impressed by the simplicity of the room. After I presented our recommendations, I knew I had impressed him, too, but I didn't know why. "Mr. Hearle," he finally said with a kindly tone, "those are very interesting ideas. Very interesting. The last time we tried something like this was in the 14th century."

Ed Hearle, a retired senior vice president, often told this story in training sessions.

The late 1970s and early 1980s saw widespread innovations in new computer, communications, and energy moving into an everyday life that pulsed to a disco beat. Windmill farms supplemented fossil fuels and nuclear power as energy sources, John Travolta got down on the dance floor, mobile telephones transcended the limits of land lines, and computers began automating tasks of all kinds. Meanwhile, gas prices skyrocketed in the mid-1970s and the stock market languished in the doldrums until 1982.

U.S. government called upon Booz Allen to help lay the groundwork for agencies dealing with new problems such as energy policy and environmental legislation. Military leaders, meanwhile, came out of Vietnam with a sense of the need to change, especially as computer and communication technologies became available to connect aircraft, vehicles, sensors, and armaments. The military reorganized its technology initiatives under the name C-cubed, for communications, command, and control (a fourth "C" was later added for "computing"), and Booz Allen reorganized its government consulting business along similar lines.

In the early 1970s, after cutbacks had forced layoffs of more than 300 staff people, a senior partner in the government consulting business named Bill Sommers visited some of Booz Allen's more successful competitors in that arena to see what they were doing differently. "I came back," he recalls, "and said, 'We've got to do more technology work. We've got to hire some ex-military people who know their way around. And we need to be cost competitive.' Two weeks later, Charlie Bowen called me and put me in charge of Booz Allen Applied Research. At age 37 I got a chance to put my money where my mouth was." And indeed, those changes set the stage for a steady growth curve and, even as BAARINC was folded back into the firm, its successor, WTB, continues on a steady growth trajectory to this day.

In the mid- and late-1970s Booz Allen consultants helped the Department of Defense determine the best training media for teaching soldiers to operate complex aircraft. They helped merge shipboard computer and communications technologies for the Navy; this project led to the development of the programmable link adapter, a device that in real time evaluates the quality of different radio and satellite communication links, and automatically chooses the best one for particular conditions. Booz Allen also was involved in communications security, including cryptographic devices, network protection, and other ways of ensuring government telecommunications. "Electronics had advanced to the point where you could build relatively small devices that were efficient in encryption and decryption," recalls Senior Vice President Ted Shema.

"The business grew," Senior Vice President Joseph Nemec Jr. says, "because we were highly incentivized. We had meetings every Monday morning in New York, where we would ask each other: 'What are you going to sell this week?' If you didn't sell, we would not eat." The pressure was relentless. Farley, who preferred face-to-face meetings to the telephone, seemed to be everywhere, egging people on.

Booz Allen repaid the initial $6 million debt within a year, and within two years annual billings had increased more than 20 percent, from $60 million to $73 million. Meanwhile, a visionary group of partners set out to ensure that the institution would be safeguarded in the future, putting it on the path to continuity and growth. They created a robust governance structure that protected the firm from external circumstances and prevented any small group of partners with

concentrated ownership from sending Booz Allen in the wrong strategic direction. No one person could own more than 3 percent of the shares, the firm's senior management was not allowed to hold a majority of seats on the board of directors, board members' terms were limited to three years, and for the first time in its history Booz Allen created a five-year plan for developing new business. This governance structure enabled the orderly transfer of ownership from one generation to the next and remains in place today.

The Chrysler Turnaround

In the late 1970s the assumed rules of business turned topsy-turvy. The price of oil, the most stable of commodities, soared. Japanese manufacturers challenged Detroit's automakers on quality. An upstart telephone company won the right to connect devices to the telephone network over the heretofore-insurmountable objections of AT&T. Two Harvard undergrads, Bill Gates and Paul Allen, created a tiny business in their dorm room that would later become Microsoft. Furthermore, business itself suddenly became not just a utilitarian but an intellectual endeavor. Between 1971 and 1981 the number of people earning MBA degrees in the United States more than doubled, from about 26,000 to 57,000. Consulting firms no longer held a monopoly on management and financial knowledge; they had to be both resourceful and nimble to keep ahead of their clients.

This was an age of strategy, in which people who shifted the direction of large

Lee Iacocca, CEO of Chrysler Motors during the early 1980s, announced in a 1983 press conference that Chrysler had paid off its federally guaranteed loans. Booz Allen's role as a consultant helped Iacocca lead Chrysler's famous recovery.

companies could become public heroes. The most visible of these in the early 1980s, as it happened, had his career linked to Booz Allen. His name was Lee Iacocca.

Chrysler was in serious trouble in 1979. The company could barely pay suppliers and creditors, it had cut its staff to the bone, and it was sitting on a perilously excessive inventory. Dealers, fearing they'd be stuck with cars they couldn't sell, were ready to abandon the brand. But Chrysler, its 4,700 dealers, and 19,000 suppliers employed a total of almost a half-million people, and U.S. President Jimmy Carter didn't want the company to sink, especially just before an election year.

Former CEO Jim Farley recalls being approached by Chrysler's board to help it prepare a reqest that the U.S. government guarantee $750 million in loans from several major banks. Treasury Secretary G. William Miller, considering the proposal, turned to Booz Allen for further help. Would that cash influx be enough for the car company to regain its viability? Led by now-retired Vice Chairman Cyrus Freidheim Jr., who once had worked at Ford, a Booz Allen team had two weeks to evaluate the company's plan. But Chrysler had no plan. Its leaders seemed to think the money alone would suffice. Nor did anyone—except for Iacocca, who had just come to Chrysler from Ford—want to hear about change; the company had already fired one investment bank, Salomon Brothers, for criticizing it. The Booz Allen team, believing that Chrysler should eliminate one of its three product platforms and cut its break-even point in half, reported that the company would be difficult to rescue, but it agreed to help with an attempted turnaround under three conditions: that Chrysler rehire Salomon Brothers, that Iacocca be made CEO, and that, as Freidheim recalled, "Iacocca personally calls Booz Allen and asks us to do the job."

According to Freidheim, it took Iacocca—known for his fierce will and independence—three weeks to pick up the phone. Ultimately, the government approved a $1.5 billion loan guarantee, and Booz Allen took on a complex advisory role, overseeing Chrysler's recovery process and periodically affirming that the Treasury Department could safely release more money to Chrysler. Meanwhile, Iacocca drove the turnaround. He talked unions into concessions, dealers into extending payments, and the buying public into reconsidering the product line. He raised $300 million by selling assets. He brought in quality production people, many of them from Ford, and promoted innovative new models such as the minivan. He symbolically passed up his own salary and visibly demonstrated that American manufacturing could regain its pride. In 1983 Chrysler paid off the last of its guaranteed loans, seven years ahead of schedule.

At Booz Allen, the consultants on the Chrysler job became the nucleus of an informal but influential group of auto-industry consultants. Other specialized practices soon began to emerge within the firm—banking, telecommunications, energy, all fueled by consultants' informal contact with each other and by the knowledge that every so often a company like Chrysler spins out

onto the knife edge of survival. In those moments, an outside view and a few sharp people can make all the difference.

Shifts in the Wind

Retired Senior Vice President Pierre Rodocanachi, a medalist on the French fencing team in the 1964 Olympics in Tokyo, joined Booz Allen in the mid-1970s in the Paris office. One of his early assignments was to head a European team working for General Electric. Its CEO, Reginald Jones, had asked Booz Allen why its Japanese competitors were introducing products more quickly and with greater flexibility than GE. What was wrong with his system? The team, headed by Senior Vice President Bill Sommers, interviewed a couple dozen of the world's leading companies in the United States, Europe, and Japan, and prepared an extensive report benchmarking all dimensions of GE activities against those companies. To present these findings, the team met with Jones on a Friday afternoon at GE's headquarters in Connecticut. To Rodocanachi's surprise, Sommers showed no slides depicting any of the benchmarking statistics. Instead, he said, "It's clear, Reg, that GE is already investing enough money in R&D. It has the right kind of people and processes." What then, Jones wanted to know, was the problem?

"Reg," said Sommers, "the problem is you." Jones's strengths—his financial background, charisma, and visibility—had influenced the entire company away from long-term development and toward shorter-term

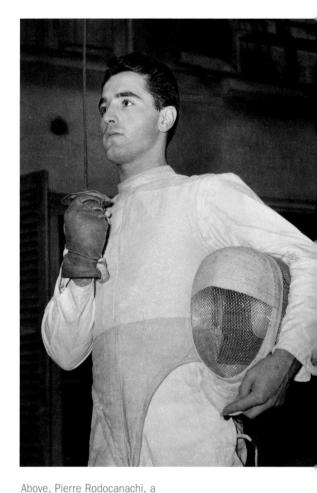

Above, Pierre Rodocanachi, a retired Booz Allen senior vice president, was a member of the French fencing team at the 1964 Summer Olympic Games in Tokyo. Left, the James J. Allen Center for Executive Education at Northwestern University is named for Booz Allen co-founder Jim Allen, who was a board member and benefactor of Northwestern's Kellogg School of Management.

reflections

By Chuck Allison

Back in the winter of 1972, I got an emergency call from Zurich. The chairman of a large multinational company asked me to be in Switzerland the next day by 11 a.m. for a meeting of the board of directors. The question was, Who should be the U.S. subsidiary's next president?

I grabbed my overnight bag, dashed to the St. Louis airport, chartered a small plane to Chicago, and jumped on the evening flight to Zurich. Early the next morning I landed in Zurich, slightly groggy, and was then off by taxi to a downtown hotel to rest, freshen up, and prepare. It was 8 a.m. What a shock when I saw myself in the mirror! My suit looked as though I had slept in it for three days. What to

do? I remembered an old technique my father had used: hang your coat and trousers on the shower rod in the hotel bathroom. Turn on the hot water in the bathtub. Shut the bathroom door and let the wrinkles steam away.

I got the process under way and flopped on my hotel bed for a ten-minute rest. I fell asleep and woke up, not ten minutes but an hour later, at nine o'clock. I jumped off the bed and groped around for my suit in the steam-choked bathroom. It was soaking, sopping, saturated

wet. With only a couple of hours left, I had to improvise. Luckily I had a balcony overlooking Lake Zurich. So I hung my coat and trousers on the railing and flopped down on the bed for

["My suit was melting before their eyes. Drip. Drip. Drip."]

another quick cat-nap. Again, I over-napped. Perhaps one hour later I woke up with a start and scrambled to get ready. Shower, shave, fresh shirt, then out to the balcony for my suit. It was frozen—stiff as a board. I had no choice: scraping and stretching, straining and tugging, I finally got inside it.

It was now 10:30, thirty minutes before meeting time. I walked like a wooden soldier. Every time I moved, my suit gave off little tinkling noises. Since our Swiss client's office

was only three blocks from my hotel, I decided to go by foot. My suit crunched as the ice crystals began to break up. I made it just in time, at one minute before 11 o'clock (a Booz Allen partner is never late). I was ushered into the boardroom to confer with 12 solemn Swiss directors, none of whom I had met before.

As I nervously neared the conclusion of my report, I began to feel damp. My suit was melting before their eyes. Drip. Drip. Drip. Puddles formed on the floor, on my chair, and on the boardroom tabletop. My Swiss friends were mesmerized. Eventually I could stand it no longer. I stopped the presentation, took a deep breath, and said, "Gentlemen, I began this presentation with a slight problem. I had only one suit, and this morning it froze. I will shortly end this presentation with a somewhat larger problem. My frozen suit is thawing. I think you deserve an explanation." Then I blurted out the whole silly chain of events.

I have rarely seen a group of men laugh so hard. The chairman patted me on the back and said, "This has been a most interesting and entertaining presentation." Then he invited me to join the board for lunch. That crazy meeting turned out to be the beginning of a fruitful relationship with our fine Swiss client. The moral is: You can still win clients, even when you're all wet.

Charles "Chuck" Allison is a retired Booz Allen senior vice president who was based in Chicago. He recorded a video version of this story, which he often told at training sessions.

financial management. "As long as this culture prevails at GE, you will always be beaten by competitors who take more risks," Sommers said.

Jones clearly did not like that answer any more than Montgomery Ward's Sewell Avery had when he heard it from Ed Booz 30 years before. But he didn't throw the consultants out, as Avery had; instead, he asked them to return on Monday morning. Jones opened that meeting by saying, "I've given it a lot of thought, and you're right." He recognized the importance of finding a successor who would make R&D the company's growth engine, a role that would require vision and imagination. Ultimately, Jack Welch was appointed as Jones's successor.

The situations at GE and Chrysler typified the challenges that faced companies in almost every industry in the late 1970s. Often, as Booz Allen found out in work for AT&T, Amoco, and others at the time, the mandate was simple but tough: adapt to new realities or stagnate. Financial services firms were no longer local retail operations. Globalization, new technologies including the automated teller machine, and new types of financial vehicles, such as the money-market fund, forced them to become more customer-oriented and sophisticated. Energy companies were no longer primarily commodities businesses; supply and demand were far less predictable. Oil companies and power utilities alike had to develop frugal, adaptive management styles, shifting with the markets and prices, and offering new kinds of value-added services and products, such as convenience stores located in gas

stations. Telecommunications companies were no longer monopolies: the pressure of new technologies, including computers and mobile phones, led to a sweeping U.S. Justice Department antitrust suit against AT&T in the late 1970s that was settled in a consent decree in 1982. Given a choice— either provide local telephone service or manufacture equipment and own the long-distance network—AT&T spun off its local service providers into seven regional firms, the "Baby Bells." Booz Allen became adept at helping companies recognize and come to terms with such inexorable shifts in their markets.

Every industry had its version of the story. Managers tested their conventional theories about how the world worked and, as often as not, found those theories wanting. It was a ripe environment for solutions, expertise, theories, even fads. One result was the business book as best-seller; another was that consulting firms discovered they had more to gain by propagating intellectual property than by keeping their ideas secret.

Supply Chain Management

Most businesses, at heart, are chains of supply logistics. Materials and capital enter the system, skilled labor transforms them step by step into goods, and these ultimately flow through distributors on their way to customers. Traditional business models divide these steps, assigning a separate organization to administer each one. Often, however, inventories accumulate at each threshold, the price of managing handoffs is

This 1981 issue of *Byte*, then the pre-eminent personal computer magazine, featured the first advertisement for VisiCalc, the first spreadsheet program. "It was mind-blowing," recalls Senior Vice President David Newkirk, who used VisiCalc on an early Apple computer. "We had been accustomed to working on big accountants' spreadsheets, with dozens of rows. If you changed one assumption, you had to recalculate the whole page by hand. Now we could change a single number and it would cascade through the P&L and balance sheet. We could model pricing or market-share change and get an eye-opening sense of how the business actually worked over time."

As the firm increased in size, partners like Senior Vice President Joyce Doria increasingly took on key roles. Doria, who specializes in organizational development and change management, was among the first women hired as a government consultant and the first female partner in the Worldwide Technology Business.

high, and conflicts among the organizations develop.

Around 1979, while consulting on a logistics and production-planning project at Dutch electronics giant Philips, Booz Allen consultant Keith Oliver—currently a senior vice president—noticed that different players in the supply chain had inherently clashing interests. For example, manufacturing wanted long lead times and large batch sizes for efficiency, while marketing, to meet customer demand flexibly, wanted variety, immediate response to change, and short batch sizes. Traditional financial processes like inventory management and budgeting,

along with computer-control systems such as materials-requirement planning and scheduling systems, reinforced this silo mindset, organization, and operation.

Influenced by Massachusetts Institute of Technology professor Jay Forrester's work on system dynamics and by Japanese management techniques, Oliver proposed that Philips convene cross-functional groups to redesign the flow of work and associated decision processes, "as if the chain of supply were a single entity, not a group of disparate functions." A Philips executive suggested he call this "supply-chain management (SCM)." The phrase "supply chain" now came to mean the flow of products and services from raw material to consumer end-product, and eventually to recycled or discarded waste.

SCM found success at Philips, Cadbury Schweppes, and other companies in Booz Allen pilots that were based on three principles articulated by Oliver: resolve functional conflicts, treat the asset base as one holistic system, and design computer systems to reflect the supply-chain structure (not the other way around). Other realizations emerged later. Among them was that meeting production and supply deadlines consistently was more important to supply-chain harmony than setting high quotas and meeting them only half the time.

The success of SCM fit well with an explicit strategy that Booz Allen undertook around this time to promote its intellectual property. In 1980 the firm published *Outlook*, the first in a series of management magazines ultimately leading to today's strategy+business, which was launched in 1995. Additionally, the late Vice President Bob Mayer convened a small working group, including leading operations academics, to talk about intellectual capital and management ideas. Booz Allen was reoccupying its original intellectual niche on the edge where ideas met action.

"Make the Client's Mission Your Mission"

In the mid-1980s Navy communications officer John Anthony Walker Jr. was arrested for selling classified Navy documents to the Soviet KGB, having severely compromised military data communications. This led to a new wave of computer-security initiatives, which Booz Allen helped manage. As computer networks proliferated and communication systems converged, point-to-point communication security evolved into a broad-based quest for information security, no matter what the delivery network, and for computer systems that could analyze and organize the flood of data collected by government agencies. Localized agencies such as police, fire, and National Guard units used these technologies in emergency-preparedness systems for natural disasters and potential attacks. To Ralph Shrader, currently Booz Allen's chairman and CEO but at the time a vice president in the government group, public-sector assignments of the era had a common mission—"to look at the old way the agency did business, to look at the possibilities given new technology, and to help build a bridge from the old to the new way."

In 1990, when Bill Stasior became chief operating officer of Booz Allen—he'd later go on to serve as chairman and CEO from 1991 to 1999—he flew to Florida to meet with General Wayne Allan Downing, director of the U.S. Army Special Operations Command, for a client's-eye assessment of a classified consulting engagement. The general arrived flanked by officers in military gear. Obviously, they all had just come straight from a paratrooper exercise. Taken aback by the fierceness of their appearance, Stasior was relieved when the general said, "We thought we'd hired just another contractor, but you guys have come in and already had a tremendous impact. Your people are making our mission their mission." That became the firm's flagship line for describing its commitment to government clients. "What

The first Earth Day was held in the United States in 1970 (shown above is the 1990 celebration in Washington, D.C.), just as an environmental consciousness began to take root, fueled by accidents at Love Canal and Three Mile Island, and supported by federal legislation such as Superfund and an amended Clean Air Act.

"We thought we'd hired just another contractor, but you guys have come in and already had a tremendous impact. Your people are making our mission their mission."

are we doing here?" Stasior would ask. "Are we making their mission our mission?"

Unifying Emergency Response

Back in 1980, in the wake of the Iranian hostage crisis, U.S. President Carter had asked a simple question with a complex answer: How would dozens of federal agencies, branches of the military, private industries, local governments, and emergency workers scattered over 50 states coordinate evacuations, restoration of power, or other emergency measures in the event of a nuclear attack? Concerned, he ordered that fast, reliable, and secure communication links be established among agencies charged with national security.

In fact, the government's emergency systems were already interconnected through the country's main telecommunications network—with voice and data traffic traveling (invisibly and inaccessible to ordinary citizens) through the same wires and switches as conventional phone calls. But because each agency had its own technical specifications and arrangements with AT&T, the sys-

tems were incompatible with each other; thus integrating them was next to impossible. Furthermore, most of the agencies had never seen any need to link directly with each other, as they reported up separate chains of command.

This was not the first time the government had tried to solve this problem. In 1962, spurred by the Cuban Missile Crisis, U.S. President John F. Kennedy created the National Communications System (NCS) within the Defense Department for this purpose. It had been working on the problem to no avail for almost 20 years. Carter's order increased NCS' funding and charged it with finding a solution.

NCS issued a request for proposals to create an emergency communication system that would cover 30 or more military and civilian organizations. As it happened, Booz Allen had just taken on a principal who understood the project's implications. Luke Capone, a former Navy admiral with a background in telecommunications, was looking to make his mark on the firm. Capone, now a retired senior vice president, joined with Ralph Shrader, who became the officer in charge

of the winning NCS proposal. Shrader led the business strategy and orals presentation team.

Almost immediately, however, the complexity of the assignment jumped by an order of magnitude: AT&T settled its antitrust suit with the Justice Department, giving up sole control of the entire nationwide phone system. This forced the government to deal with eight smaller phone companies and myriad subcontractors rather than one. Bringing all the relevant firms and agencies together was a dizzying prospect.

But NCS had a key asset—a visionary leader. General William "Bill" Hillsman, one of the youngest three-star generals in the military, reported to both the Pentagon and the White House, having recognized the need for sponsorship by both. In a precursor to a structure now commonly used to manage collaboration between the public and private sectors, Hillsman, with Booz Allen's help, convened a National Security Telecommunications Advisory Committee (NSTAC) whose job was make recommendations on policies of emergency preparedness and related issues. Including the CEOs of 17 telecommunications companies plus key officials in the relevant government agencies, this committee became the arena for negotiating difficult issues in the reconstruction of the emergency communication network, including the highly sensitive question of how different companies would be paid for their work.

Dennis O. Doughty, who led the firm's NCS team during the late 1990s and is now president of the Worldwide Technology Business, recalls, "At first no one wanted to give an inch. Government organizations were vying for control of the underlying assets, private competitors were fighting hammer and tong for customers, and both groups were eyeing each other and wondering, 'Are you trying to pull something over on me?' But as we kept talking, people began to operate out of a commitment toward a common goal and a common good."

Development of the NCS system began in 1983 and has evolved ever since. Ultimately its greatest test came on September 11, 2001, when terrorists attacked the World Trade Center in New York. The attack destroyed major pieces of the New York–New England region's telephone and cell-phone infrastructure, located in the trade center, all but completely severing public telephone service. The Government Emergency Telecommunications Service, an access-code–based backup network that is part of the NCS system built with Booz Allen's help, enabled some segments of the emergency response community to communicate when other channels failed. Furthermore, NCS made it possible for the Federal Aviation

Ensuring Pipeline Safety

After the tanker Exxon *Valdez* spilled nearly 11 million gallons of crude oil into Prince William Sound in 1989, Booz Allen was asked to recommend ways to make the Alyeska Pipeline in Alaska more secure against spills. Joyce Doria, now a Booz Allen senior vice president, managed the assignment, traveling to Prudhoe Bay in minus-72-degree weather to inspect the pipeline firsthand.

"You have to wear special clothes, and if your bare hands touch a piece of metal, they stick," she recalls. "In the briefing, they told me to urinate on my hand if I got stuck. They weren't used to having women up there."

In a subsequent assignment, a Booz Allen team discovered some irregularities. The team recommended a new oversight mechanism involving representatives from the federal Interior, Transportation, and Energy departments. The new structure eventually was implemented despite fierce political opposition.

In the 1980s, as systems of many kinds became increasingly computerized, Booz Allen used its engineering expertise to help clients monitor and manage complex infrastructures for power, water, and security. Above, an engineer at the controls of a power station in the United Kingdom.

Administration and the Air Force to order the grounding of virtually every flight in U.S. airspace within minutes of the attack. Today the NCS is a critical component of the Department of Homeland Security, and it remains a Booz Allen client.

The Evolution of Government

The use of computers made it possible in the 1970s and 1980s to model water, power, traffic, electric, transportation, and other large-scale systems with unprecedented complexity and adaptability. Local, regional, and national governments worldwide found their roles changing from controller/operators of systems to regulator/mediators of large-scale systems involving a multitude of providers—and Booz Allen increasingly played a part in helping clients through these transitions.

In Europe, Booz Allen undertook a number of intensive projects helping many formerly government-run operations—generally in the telecommunications and energy sectors—become fully independent, market-driven private companies.

In the United States, Booz Allen helped the Federal Aviation Administration create a new certification program for air-traffic controllers and pilots, the Treasury Department change the way it designs and produces money, and the federal court system revamp its scheduling process. Local city governments, starting with a prototype in Wichita Falls, Texas, used computers to pull together information about tax rolls, land surveys, police records, fire safety, and quality of life. In the 1970s "Transbus" project, the U.S. Urban

Mass Transportation Administration and several vehicle manufacturers worked with Booz Allen to rethink how buses were designed; the wheelchair-accessible buses on today's city streets owe their existence to that project.

One catalyst for change in government was the environmental movement. Heather Burns, now a Booz Allen senior vice president, joined the firm in the early 1970s to co-found an environmental consulting practice. In 1978 toxic chemicals from an industrial waste dump near Love Canal in Niagara Falls, New York, bubbled into a children's playground—sparking Congress to create the Superfund program in an effort to find and clean up the nation's worst hazardous-waste sites. Booz Allen helped plan Superfund's administration, including the setup of programs for toxicity evaluation, title searches, finance, and community relations. Burns recalls, "I met people whose kids were dying of cancer. This was a very tough assignment." Despite controversial moments, the U.S. Environmental Protection Agency (EPA), which has managed Superfund since its creation, has been credited with bringing the public, government, and industry together to craft pragmatic solutions even under emotionally charged circumstances. Booz Allen later ended up helping the EPA integrate its enforcement databases so the agency could track permits, emissions, and violations comprehensively.

McCullough's Big Changes

Jim Farley retired as chairman in 1985. Characteristically, he set up a committee to search for and pick his successor. The man the committee chose was R. Michael "Mike" McCullough, the firm's first CEO to come from the government side of the business. He had a remarkable memory and was known as a mentor who would go to great lengths to help his protégés. Farley's committee had singled him out as someone who would make important changes, and not necessarily popular ones. In fact, his tenure, from 1985 to 1990, coincided with a stormy chapter in Booz Allen history, as internal conflicts—between the commercial and government sides of the firm, between regions, and within offices—surfaced frequently. Yet this was also a period of substantial growth, particularly in government consulting. In the end, McCullough would be remembered primarily for making three major changes.

First, he broke up the fiefdoms of the firm's regional offices, making Booz Allen unique as a consulting firm that delivered its services primarily through specialized sectors aligned to those in industry and government. This improved the quality and consistency with which Booz Allen could serve global corporations and other clients spanning regions, plus it improved collaboration among regional partners who formerly competed with one another. At the same time, a functional orientation focused on in-depth, cross-industry implementation projects (such as supply chain management, information technology, and operations) became an additional source of strength for the firm. Facing the market along industry lines and functional lines, instead of geographic ones, opened the door to more client-centered con-

sultations. No other consulting firm had ever brought that combination of sector and functional expertise to executive-level strategic consultation.

McCullough's second major change involved partners' compensation. The system he inherited had been set up to encourage rainmaking at a time when the firm badly needed cash. Bonuses were set by a compensation committee based on the size of a partner's billings and anything else that happened to matter to the committee that year. If there were 150 partners, there might be 150 different bonuses, each with its own hurried rationale. "The new concept was very simple," McCullough recalls. "We'd try to make the pie bigger instead of competing over the size of the slices." With then-Vice President Andy Messina, McCullough installed a series of partnership levels and a point system to allocate bonuses to each. The size of the bonus was set by the performance of the entire firm. Partners now had a built-in incentive to encourage each others' success, to seek business together, to collaborate on behalf of client needs, and to cultivate trust. Dan Lewis, currently president of Booz Allen's Worldwide Commercial Business, credits this system with the firm's resilience in several crises. Says Lewis: "You can't survive in this compensation scheme unless you're playing for the institution as a whole."

For his third major change, McCullough lowered the financial hurdles and requirements for setting up international offices. To be sure, Booz Allen had been doing international work, usually cultivated by a handful of

R. Michael McCullough, CEO of Booz Allen between 1985 and 1990, led three structural changes that laid the groundwork for the firm's current success: a shift from region-based to function-driven organization, a new compensation system, and an expansion in international activity.

consultants. In the late 1970s, for example, Saudi Arabia had hired Booz Allen to help design the institutional framework for the new industrial cities of Jubail and Yanbu, to house tens of thousands of expatriates working in the country's oil and petro-chemicals industry. But throughout his tenure as chairman Jim Farley had been clear that neither people nor money were available to invest in a full commitment to the international business, and Booz Allen thus had no strategy for international growth. By 1984, however, the time had come to establish a deliberate global pres-ence. A number of new offices opened around the world, especially in Europe, and the firm escalated its local recruiting to fill them. Rather than hiring people who were well-connected to local aristocracies, as some other firms did, Booz Allen sought people who were open-minded and capable of dealing with a variety of cultures.

Düsseldorf set the pace, expanding into the German-speaking areas of Austria and Switzerland. Senior Vice President Helmut Meier recalls that Senior Vice President Gerd Wittkemper "was the cornerstone. He was brought in to this fragile, little German struc-ture at that time, and he built an extremely successful partner crew around him." Booz Allen took on projects for some of the largest corporations in Germany: Daimler-Benz, Lufthansa, and Deutsche Bank. This work would lead to efforts in the late 1990s and into 2000 to help MTV develop a German-language version. Vice President Adam Bird explained, "Music tastes are not international; they're local. MTV had a global

brand, but to be successful they had to have a multi-local presence. Today MTV International is very Italian in Italy, very German in Germany, and very local in the U.K."

The MTV job represented one of the first major consulting assignments in the growing field of international media. RadioTeleLuxembourg (RTL), a European radio and advertising company with a small TV station, began to explore satellite-direct television. Retired Senior Vice President Pierre Rodocanachi recalls that a seemingly simple Booz Allen project for RTL brought together a variety of complex and interre-lated issues—the life expectancy of transis-tors on satellites, the ability to focus a sig-nal onto the footprint of Europe, dish sizes, government restrictions, the willingness of customers to pay monthly fees, the viability of advertising, and the potential sources of movies, sports, and other programming. Rodocanachi says, "Ultimately this move pushed the industry to consolidate around a number of key players, one of whom is RTL today."

As Munich-based Vice President Christian Burger notes, Booz Allen's offices were set up consciously as portals into a global enter-prise. The combined Booz Allen culture and expanding computing infrastructure enabled far higher levels of cross-continental collabo-ration. "I can open the door of the office in Stockholm or Madrid and within minutes, I have an office, access to the global network, and I can become productive," Burger says. "The business process is geared toward seamless international presence."

In the late 20th century technology appeared in unlikely places, such as this pastoral scene in the German countryside, as satellite dishes, cell-phone transponders, and fiber optics expanded the global reach of voice and data communication.

Waves of Transformation

Booz Allen faced an identity crisis as the 1990s opened, when tensions between two very different approaches to consulting came to a boil. The commercial practice—dominant in most Booz Allen offices—focused on private-sector clients, employing a comparatively small staff of consultants to provide strategic advice to top decision makers. The public-sector practice—housed primarily in an expanding complex in Bethesda, Maryland, just outside Washington, D.C.—served the military and other government agencies. This part of Booz Allen typically engaged in in-depth, long-term projects in which consultants helped agencies plan for, evaluate, implement, and coordinate increasingly complex and technologically advanced systems.

The commercial business had its roots in the business strategy arena (most commercial consultants, by now, held MBA degrees from exclusive business schools like Harvard, Stanford, Wharton, and Northwestern); Booz Allen competed head-on with McKinsey, Boston Consulting Group, and Bain for assignments advising CEOs on restructuring, mergers, and competitive distinction. They were, in effect, heirs to the style established by Ed Booz and Jim Allen in the 1930s. They often worked alone or in very small teams, traveled frequently, consulted on a short-term basis in many cases, and often operated entirely at their own discretion and that of the client.

By contrast, the public-sector consulting practice traced its roots to the Navy and Air Force work of the 1940s and 1950s. Projects tended to involve large teams of technically trained specialists from a wide variety of backgrounds who stayed largely in one locale. There were hundreds of employees at the Bethesda office alone by the early 1990s, most working on only one long-term project at a time for the U.S. government. The public-sector teams had to operate within strict regulatory constraints, generally competing against other technology consulting firms like EDS (Electronic Data Systems), SAIC (Science Applications International Corporation), and CSC Index (the management consulting arm of Computer Sciences Corporation).

To a few partners on the commercial side of Booz Allen, the technology business was "not strategic": its nitty-gritty public-sec-

tor work, they felt, would gradually erode the cachet and thus the marketability of Booz Allen. They believed the government business could tarnish the brand and that it was distracting the firm from corporate strategic consulting, its flagship mission as they saw it. Some partners argued that Booz Allen should spin off or sell the government consulting business. Other partners, however, saw synergy. According to their view, the two practices had much to learn from each other, and because of the cyclical nature of consulting, each practice could help buffer the firm against downturns in the other's business cycle. Furthermore, a few Booz Allen partners saw a trend emerging, albeit in a nascent form: clients in both the private and public sectors were beginning to demand solutions that called for skills from both sides of the firm. Why, they asked, couldn't Booz Allen build bridges between its practices, and set the stage for a kind of success that other consulting firms could only envy?

Emotions ran high, and amid the intensity a movement arose for a change in leadership. In 1991 Mike McCullough stepped down and William "Bill" Stasior was voted the firm's new chairman and chief executive officer. Having held many senior governance and management positions at Booz Allen, he was a unifying choice. He quickly made it clear where he stood on the identity debate: a few months after becoming CEO he reorganized the varied Booz Allen commercial and government businesses into two units, the Worldwide Commercial Business (WCB), serving primarily the corporate sector, and the Worldwide Technology Business (WTB),

serving government. This gave both practices legitimacy and allowed each to proceed with its own business model, unimpeded by the other.

The Stasior Era

Slim, bespectacled, balding, and moustached, Bill Stasior had an affinity for consensus, but also a plain-spoken directness, a tough but good-humored way of cutting to the heart of an issue. At one top meeting, several board members questioned whether a compensation-review team might play favorites; they insisted that Stasior sit in on their meetings to keep things fair. He refused to micromanage them. "The team's job is to work in the best interest of the firm," he said. "If they can't do that job, then we'll consider replacing them."

Stasior viewed social issues in a similarly straightforward way. Eschewing de rigueur contributions to national philanthropies, he leveraged the firm's greatest asset—the expertise of its staff—in two ways. He encouraged Booz Allen people to work on community-service projects and supported them with matching grants; thousands of employees at all levels of Booz Allen have since volunteered for organizations ranging from soup kitchens to community theater to youth services to Habitat for Humanity. Stasior further committed the firm to public service by offering pro bono consultations, which have since helped transform a variety of organizations—from small businesses in Harlem, New York, to the Special Olympics. In a practice that continues to this day,

William Stasior, chairman and CEO of Booz Allen during the 1990s, encouraged and set a tone for community involvement at all levels of the firm. This photograph shows him with the Environmental Science Club of Paul Junior High School, an inner-city charter school in Washington, D.C.

teams of Booz Allen consultants approach these pro bono assignments in the same way they do paid work.

Booz Allen has worked for more than seven years with the Special Olympics, which provides sports training and athletic competitions for more than one million children and adults worldwide with disabilities. In 2000, for example, Senior Vice President Bruce Pasternack and Vice President Joni Bessler led a Booz Allen team that helped the Special Olympics adapt its organizational structure, increase its leadership capabilites, develop meaningful metrics, and create an information-technology strategy.

Booz Allen's involvement in community service reverberates worldwide—in Germany, for instance, in a set of arts events under the name *Macht:Kultur* (which loosely translates as "the power of" or "be active in" culture). The events include salons where businesspeople from a number of companies discuss a wide range of issues and ideas with community leaders and artists. "The only rule," says Senior Vice President Helmut Meier, "is that we cannot talk about business."

As CEO, Stasior took visible stands on diversity inside and outside of the firm. He championed antidiscrimination policies, played an active role on the Executive Committee of the United Negro College Fund, spoke at the Working OUT conference for gay and lesbian MBAs, and gained management backing to extend benefits to same-sex and opposite-sex domestic partners of Booz Allen's employees. His philosophy was best expressed in a speech entitled

Reggie Van Lee, a Booz Allen senior vice president, left, was principal for a day at a New York area high school. Below, Booz Allen volunteers help decorate pumpkins at the Fall Festival at Camp Friendship, a Maryland-based camp for children with cancer.

Above, a Booz Allen senior associate poses with some of the kids at Santa Fe, a shelter for abandoned children in São Paolo, Brazil.

"Do the Right Thing" at the firm's first Diversity Awards Dinner in 1998. Stasior argued that it's essential to "recognize that doing the right thing is a lot more than not doing the wrong thing." He observed that most people do not purposely discriminate in hiring or promotions, nor make racist or sexist remarks. "But far fewer people are really doing the right thing in terms of *actively* making a difference…going beyond good intentions to make good things happen."

Stasior believed that doing the right thing was compatible with the firm's increasingly diverse staff and with its business interests—its clients, too, were more diverse. If Booz Allen couldn't provide teams as diverse and open as the people they advised, the firm would lose its relevance, he believed. In the early 1990s, a team of vice presidents (led by Paul Anderson and Chuck Allison) reworked the firm's employee-development strategy. They created programs for the advancement of minorities and women, anti-sexual-harassment policies, and peer appraisal systems, plus a set of leadership, professional-development, and human-relationship-management courses. Over three years all but two of Booz Allen's partners attended a program of two week-long Aspen Institute sessions moderated by James O'Toole, a well-known expert on organizational leadership and the author of *Values-Based Leadership*.

Stasior often quoted Arie de Geus: "It's the walking that beats the path, not the path that beats the walk." This line, based on a poem by Antonio Machado, reflected Stasior's belief that there was no predefined destination, that small choices made along the way would establish the firm's direction. A flurry of events underlined the unpredictability of the future. Japan seemed poised to overtake the U.S. economy. Then it faltered. The Berlin Wall fell. The Soviet Union unraveled. Apartheid abruptly ended in South Africa. And when Saddam Hussein's Iraq suddenly invaded Kuwait, the United States and its allies found themselves embroiled in a war in the Persian Gulf.

"Smart" Weapons and Interoperability

The 1991 Gulf War is still remembered for its televised images of "smart" bombs and missiles that seemed to hit their target on every shot. Computerized technology had made possible not only an entirely new, highly accurate form of precision-guided weaponry but also a new way of waging war—seemingly by remote control.

A number of partners in the Worldwide Technology Business recall that the war was a real test of the new forms of technological weaponry and military systems. A tank or gun was no longer an isolated machine; it was also a sensor, collecting information that was instantly uploaded to military computer systems where the information could be analyzed, shared, and used.

Unfortunately, the information systems were not yet fully interoperable, particularly across branches of the military. For example, the U.S. Navy and Air Force both flew airplanes, but their information systems were not coordinated. Each group therefore knew things the others didn't, and major tactical decisions were made without all of the knowledge available. When the Gulf War ended, Pentagon planners were open to crossing that divide, and Booz Allen helped as they set out to create a communications and information system that would allow service-wide data sharing and interoperability. This would be not just a matter of designing a computer system, but of providing the training, culture, and organizational structure to enable people to use it.

The imperative led ultimately to a project known as WarBreaker, prototype of a potential future military communication/information system. Under development by the Defense Advanced Research Projects Agency (DARPA) since the first Gulf War, WarBreaker linked "sensors to shooters" to detect, identify, locate, and target mobile missile launchers that could elude detection from any single reconnaissance asset; WarBreaker demonstrated that correlating data from satellites, ground- and sea-based radar, sensors, human observation, and other sources before a critical target had time to move or launch could provide an effective solution. Had WarBreaker existed in the first Gulf War, it likely could have intercepted the Scud missiles that Iraq fired against Israel, Saudi Arabia, and other Gulf nations. WarBreaker's success also created a new interactive way to simulate warfare by linking disparate simulation tools together simultaneously with human decision making.

The requirement for interoperability wasn't restricted to the military. WTB's consultants were increasingly called upon to help civilian agencies share information across boundaries. After the 1995 bombing of the Murrah Federal Building in Oklahoma City, the General Services Administration developed an information system for protecting government assets such as buildings, parks, and utilities. A network called ADNET facilitated the sharing of information by a range of federal agencies, embassies, and local law-enforcement organizations with drug-fighting missions; in 1996 ADNET-derived information led the Coast Guard's Caribbean unit to a boat loaded with four tons of cocaine. Other integrated networks improved National Guard training and emergency responsiveness, the distribution of vaccines among a variety of government agencies (coordinated by the Centers for Disease Control), and the procedures of the U.S. Senate.

Transforming an Inner City

In the mid-1990s, Washington, D.C., was known for its high crime rate. In early 1997 the District of Columbia Control Board, which then oversaw city government, awarded Booz Allen a contract for a management review of the Metropolitan Police Department (MPD). As Booz Allen Senior Vice President Gary Mather, who headed a joint WCB/WTB team that worked on the assignment, recalls, "Our objective wasn't to do another study—there had been 27 of them—but to engineer a process of driving change."

When the Booz Allen team first met then-Washington Mayor Marion Barry, he said, "You guys are from McLean [Virginia], right?" Why, he asked, shouldn't he hire a firm with

The 1990s were a time of sudden and dramatic political and social change. The Berlin Wall fell and the Soviet Union collapsed, Nelson Mandela's election as president of South Africa sealed the end of apartheid, Tiger Woods became the first African-American golf champion in the United States, and MTV—with Madonna as one of the decade's biggest new stars—reinforced the music video as a new centerpiece of Western youth culture.

The firm helped the Washington, D.C., police department transform itself in the 1990s. Booz Allen's Chips Stewart, Ron Haddock, and Gary Mather pose with Police Chief Larry Soulsby.

"Eliminate crime, fear of crime and disorder, while establishing trust and respect within the community."

offices inside the D.C. limits? Senior Vice President Fred Cipriano answered Barry's question with a key fact: hundreds of Booz Allen employees were doing volunteer and pro bono work in the district.

That hurdle overcome, the project started by giving the MPD a new mission statement: "Eliminate crime, fear of crime and disorder, while establishing trust and respect within the community." Then it tackled the critical area of officer redeployment. The MPD had maintained the same beat boundaries for more than 30 years and didn't have a strategy for redeploying people or allocating resources. A new plan redrew boundaries and set up training for all patrol officers in the techniques of crime prevention and local problem solving. The project moved hundreds of officers from back-office jobs to street patrol and reallocated more than $30 million from administrative functions to the patrol bureau.

With this new operating model in place, the overall crime rate in Washington dropped significantly—about 23 percent in 1997, the first year of the engagement, with homicides down 28 percent to the lowest rate in a decade and violent crime down 24 percent. Crime fell another 20 percent in 1998. Police take-home pay and morale rose, as did residents' satisfaction with the police department, and the redeployment helped the department save more than $20 million. Furthermore, the MPD had a new information-management system, better cooperation with agencies such as the Federal Bureau of Investigation and Drug Enforcement Administration, and a comprehensive inven-

tory of its own equipment. In 1997 Congress passed the District of Columbia Revitalization Act, modeled after the approach taken by the Control Board and Booz Allen.

A Booz Allen advisory board meeting in January 1996 included former Secretary of State Henry Kissinger, bottom, third from right.

The Triple Crown of Transformation

MIT computer-science professor Michael Hammer had coined the word "reengineering" in the mid-1980s to describe a process for combining such tools as process mapping, organizational design, and computer

> "A turning point in the transformation of the firm from mostly American to truly global was an assignment in Germany beginning in 1989."

An oil tanker plies the waters off Alaska in the 1990s, a decade in which Booz Allen helped Mobil rethink its retail business and BP and Amoco integrate following their 1998 merger.

technology into a holistic approach to reinventing the way a company does business. In many companies reengineering became a synonym for across-the-board cost-cutting and unproductive layoffs. But at its best, this kind of wholesale, full-scale process redesign provided an important tool in the reinvigoration of once-somnolent giants of the corporate world—and Booz Allen became one of its most effective practitioners. The firm deliberately went beyond reengineering, differentiating its commercial practice with a "triple crown" approach to business transformation in which a single team would offer an integrated trio of services: strategic consultation (for example, helping clients decide which product lines or divisions to promote and which to abandon), operational consultation (reworking a process flow to eliminate waste and improve productivity), and information-technology consulting (recommending computer/communication systems that would make the first two sets of change feasible).

A few of Booz Allen's strategy-oriented consultants didn't fully approve of this new approach, but it made sense to clients. It was also complex enough that it paved the way for an amplification of thought leadership among Booz Allen's consultants. Henceforth, when they showed up with a "theory of the firm" about a client company,

their view encompassed not just the client's potential for increased business or productivity gains but the relationship between the two—along with the technological underpinnings that would make the most sense given the client's industry and culture.

A mid-1990s project for Procter & Gamble, led by Chuck Allison, proved the triple crown's effectiveness. P&G had been growing aggressively worldwide but could not keep prices low enough to outflank competitors. An analysis identified the culprit—complexity in production and distribution as P&G moved into new countries and introduced new brands. P&G Chairman Edwin Artzt led a restructuring in which a P&G/Booz Allen team removed layers of management, streamlined regional businesses, revamped the company's logistics infrastructure, and accelerated technological innovation. After the restructuring, 17 pricing variables and five payment schedules in some product lines had been cut to one each. The P&G job introduced the concept of "decision rights": clarifying explicitly which executives were authorized to make which decisions for any product line, as an integral link between corporate strategy and workflow. Now, strategy did not have to be set only at the top; explicit decision rights could allow strategic choices to be made in alignment at many different levels of the hierarchy.

Senior Vice President Jack McGrath's consultation for The Goodyear Tire & Rubber Company and the Stouffer division of Nestlé demonstrated, also in the 1990s, how a comprehensive transformation could align marketing and production in new and profitable ways. Both companies had spent enormous amounts of money on promotion with little confidence in its effectiveness. By applying a combination of strategic tools such as financial analysis, computer analysis of sales and marketing data, and the redesign of work processes, each company was able for the first time to analyze the impact of its promotions on sales. Booz Allen went on to conduct similar work for The Kellogg Company, Tropicana, Clorox, Coca-Cola, Coke's Minute Maid unit, and RJR Nabisco.

A project for General Dynamics brought the same concepts to a major government contractor. Bath Iron Works, a General Dynamics facility on the coast of Maine that had built massive ships since the days of square-riggers, turned itself into a builder of state-of-the-art surface fighting vessels for the U.S. Navy. The turnaround involved a cost-reduction process, not just for boat building but for the operation and service of the ship after its construction. Each warship now contains a computerized data warehouse that tracks maintenance and deployment information, enabling significant cost savings over a vessel's lifespan.

Another commercial consulting project transformed the visible face of consumer retail. In 1992 the Mobil Oil Company asked Booz Allen to help revamp its U.S. retailing business to improve efficiency and profitability. A team of 25 consultants reconsidered every aspect of service-station operations, from the hours of operation to the potential mix of products and services to the training of employees. Following through on Booz Allen's groundwork, Mobil established the prototype of a new American retail icon: the service station/grocery/travel store with an oil company's logo as the brand identifier. As the *Washington Post* noted five years later, "The program helped turn Mobil's U.S. retailing business into the most profitable in the industry today."

Booz Allen also refined and accelerated its post-merger integration practice in the 1990s. In 1998, two large oil companies—British Petroleum and Amoco—merged to become the third largest oil company in the world. First called BP Amoco and then BP, the new company needed to bring people together to create a whole greater than the sum of its parts—with just 100 days to design a fully operational management-information and financial system before the date on which the U.S. Federal Trade Commission was scheduled to approve the merger. Using a baseline survey developed by the project team, Booz Allen gathered data from 700 parts of the new organization scattered across 120 countries, and allocated costs and headcount by function and location. A few years later, when Pfizer and Warner Lambert completed the largest merger of pharmaceutical firms in history, Booz Allen helped them use a similar transformation process to integrate two sprawling businesses into one.

The Reshaping of Europe

As Booz Allen's presence grew around the world, it established an increasingly local identity in the countries in which it did business, particularly in Europe and South America. A turning point in the transformation of Booz Allen from a mostly American to a truly global firm was an assignment that began in 1989 and lasted through most of the 1990s. It ultimately ended in an environment of widespread change to the political and cultural landscape of Germany—indeed, to much of Europe as a whole.

Toward the end of the 1980s, West Germany's Postal-Telephone-Telecommunications (PTT) ministry hired Booz Allen to assist with privatization of the country's telecom operations. The firm's job was to help a newly created company, Deutsche Telekom A.G., adjust to post-monopoly life as a competitor providing land-line telephone and data communications to homes and offices, plus long-distance and cellular phone services in Germany—and doing business outside the country for the first time.

It was as complex a project as Booz Allen consultants had ever experienced—and one of extremely high visibility. Deutsche Telekom executives needed to make the kinds of decisions—about setting up business units, identifying and targeting customer segments, and deploying new technologies such as wireless and high-speed data services—that they had never faced. Then, eight months after the engagement began, the Berlin Wall fell and the reunification

of the two Germanys became inevitable. Booz Allen's consultants saw not just an opportunity but a responsibility: the moribund businesses of the East would have to learn modern business practices fast and turn themselves around, or the economy of the former East Germany might become permanently dependent on the West.

Jürgen Peddinghaus, a now-retired Booz Allen senior vice president, spent four months touring East Germany to take an inventory of industries, scouting for candidates for acquisition or partnership with West German firms. This groundwork led to several privatization initiatives, among them the restructuring of the biggest steel manufacturer in East Germany, the Schwermaschinen-Kombinant Ernst Thälmann (SKET). But the most critical operation was Deutsche Telekom's takeover of the East German phone system. German Chancellor Helmut Kohl personally sponsored this *Telekom Aufbau Ost* (Reconstruction East) project, led by Deutsche Telekom CEO Helmut Ricke and Booz Allen Senior Vice President Klaus Mattern.

The challenges were immense. The East German phone company had been infiltrated by members of Stasi, the former regime's feared secret service. Land lines typically dated back to World War II. People who had waited ten or twelve years for a phone installation often waited hours for a dial tone. East Germany also lacked the nodes and connection points necessary for cell phone service.

One of the priorities was to find leaders from within East Germany for this new division of Deutsche Telekom. Peddinghaus led

the search. With a West German personnel executive and a legal advisor, he interviewed about 150 East German phone-company employees, trying to distinguish former Stasi spymasters from potentially viable managers. Deutsche Telekom, still a Booz Allen client, is now the third largest telecom company in the world, the owner of a leading cellular phone service (T-Mobile), and a pioneer in European broadband service.

Germany's reunification, meanwhile, bolstered by its new integrated telecommunication system, became one of the greatest triumphs of democracy in modern times. It was followed barely three years later by the coalescence of the European Union (EU). Here, too, Booz Allen played a role; EU policies called for the privatization of many government enterprises, and the firm could provide both strategic perspective and technical help. Privatization projects involved wireless telephone service in France, the government-owned railroad in Russia, and a variety of industries in Hungary, Poland, the Czech Republic, and Albania. Previous initiatives in Spain, Scandinavia, and Eastern Europe expanded. And in Italy, Booz Allen Vice Presidents Fernando Napolitano and Luigi Pugliese would in a few years begin a celebrated rethinking of digital television as a tool for transforming the nation's telecommunications infrastructure.

As Senior Vice President Rolf Habbel, now the leader of Booz Allen's European business, recalls, "One of the key elements of our success in the German-speaking area was the combination of pressure at that time with an opportunity to make something

Privatization and revitalization of once government-run industries occurred at an increasing pace in Europe, Asia, and South America in the 1990s. This involved, among other sectors, the automobile industry in East Germany, left, and the railroad in Russia. Above is a detail from a Russian rail car.

Senior Vice President Gerd Wittkemper, above, brought a spirit of teamwork and cooperation to Booz Allen's German offices when he joined the firm in 1987. His leadership was crucial to the firm's successful expansion in the German-speaking area throughout the 1990s.

happen. We became a close working team under the leadership of Gerd Wittkemper. The team stayed together with one common objective: Let's grow this business." Within Germany, a group of companies, including Daimler-Benz, Lufthansa, and Bertelsmann, became ever larger global players. In a project for the European Space Agency, Booz Allen helped coordinate 15 member nations, each speaking a different language and each with a different set of technical standards.

Later in the decade, Booz Allen expanded in northern Europe by acquiring Carta Corporate Advisors, which had a presence in all four Scandinavian countries.

Privatization in the Developing World

Booz Allen's practice in the developing world, while established in the early 1950s, took an upward turn in the 1990s on a surge in business—as well as ground-breaking projects—in Brazil, Mexico, Venezuela, Thailand, South Korea, and elsewhere in Southeast Asia. The economies of many of these countries expanded dramatically, often as governments privatized formerly state-controlled industries or opened monopolies to new competition.

In Brazil, for example, Booz Allen helped the national telephone system go from a monopoly to free competition within three years. In July 1998 the government privatized 23 state-run, regional monopolies and consolidated them into three independent competitors. One of the three, Tele Centro Sul, renamed itself Brasil Telecom and trans-

formed itself into as modern a company as can be found anywhere. It entered new businesses—Internet access, local- and wide-area network integration, call-center outsourcing, data communications, and nation-wide long distance, among others—and it focused internally on operational improvements, productivity gains, and new types of customer service. It shut down old store-fronts, the monopolies' former public face (notorious for limited hours and inconsistent, slow service), in favor of customer-focused call centers equipped to solve problems 24 hours a day.

Another key Booz Allen project in Asia involved the Thai military. With one of the so-called "tiger economies" of the early 1990s, Thailand quickly emerged as a pivotal player in Asia's expansion. In the midst of the country's growth, the Royal Thai Supreme Command undertook an ambitious modernization built around a world-class communications system and centralized control of the Army, Navy, and Air Force. In size, scope, and impact the new Thai system ranked among the most complex integration projects undertaken by Booz Allen at that time. Conceived in 1994 and implemented between 1996 and 1999, the project is credited with streamlining military decision making and improving day-to-day management, border-control and refugee operations, drug-control and antiterrorism efforts. Additionally, the project made the Thai armed forces fully interoperable with those of the United States, leading to the first-ever joint U.S.-Thai military exercises, in mid-1999, three years ahead of the government's schedule.

These projects and others represented harbingers of a sea change in the world's thinking about development. The prevailing "Washington consensus" of the 1980s and early 1990s had held that if developing countries organized their economies around Western-style free-market rules, the industrialized world could grant them development aid with reasonable expectations of return; that, then, would fuel their growth. But by the end of the 1990s it was clear that developing nations could more effectively kick-start their own economies without wholesale adoption of the culture and practices of the West. These countries defined and pursued development on their own terms, establishing a pattern for change that is still unfolding—one in which government reform, business modernization, local culture, and global interconnection reinforce each other to produce a new set of customers. They may be poor today, but they are likely tomorrow's middle class.

New Visions and Strategic Shifts

During the recession of 1991, a group of senior partners in the Worldwide Commercial Business began to look at ways to re-energize the firm and create incentives and policies to reinforce that mission. The initiative came to be known as Vision 2000, or V2K. The review turned up ingrained divisiveness. Many Booz Allen consultants often didn't share information or help each other, usually out of fear that others' mistakes would jeop-

ardize their own client relationships. Bill Stasior responded as many CEOs would—setting out some reforms by decree. But they didn't take hold. Recalls Stasior: "There wasn't any great chorus out there of belief, satisfaction, or emotional commitment." Thus, at the 1992 annual meeting in Barcelona, Spain, Stasior asked every partner to write him a letter laying out a vision for the firm. More than 80 percent replied. Now-retired Senior Vice President Chuck Lucier helped craft a new vision statement from the responses; he and Stasior went on a three-week tour of Booz Allen offices, testing and refining it into a template for a new commercial-business strategy. It was at around this time, in 1992, that Booz Allen moved into new corporate headquarters on its own campus in McLean, Virginia.

WCB introduced its new strategy in October 1993. At the same time, Brian Dickie, a partner in his 30s who was a champion of V2K, became president of WCB. Vision 2000 contained six basic principles: first, it stated that the firm wouldn't just take any client that walked in the door; rather, it would pursue clients that wanted to work with Booz Allen and that could make a difference in the world. It also set a vision of growth by expanding business lines and increasing the firm's global presence. It sought to coalesce and exploit intellectual capital scattered throughout WCB, and it fashioned a service methodology in which multidisciplinary teams would provide strategic consulting, operations, and information-technology implementation. Finally, Vision 2000 made new commitments to training,

continual learning, and community service. New policies reinforced the principles. A revised compensation formula, for example, tied bonuses in part to the collective growth of WCB, and to partner and staff review of each others' work.

As they had in the 1970s, when called upon to set a course together, the partners excelled at revitalizing their business. "Suddenly people were paying attention," Stasior says. "They were attracting clients, developing relationships, managing staff better. We had just hit the nerve of an aspiration deficit." Financial measures such as billability and partner income surged by as much as 50 percent. A less measurable but more telling indicator: practice teams asked for the right to select their team leaders. Now-retired Senior Vice President Paul Anderson designed a process for doing so. "To my amazement," Stasior said, "they always selected one of the two or three people who would have been on my list. Because their peers put the new leaders in place, they came in with a mission and weren't going to fail."

Vision 2000 recharged Booz Allen's sense of collaboration and shared intellectual property. Led by Lucier, WCB in 1994 created a computer-based information repository called Knowledge OnLine. Serving as Booz Allen's first intranet, it had two basic components: a directory of in-house experts and a consultation library containing reports, informal write-ups, codified surveys, project summaries, PowerPoint decks, proposal templates, methodologies, case studies, marketing materials, and other information from consulting engagements. A Booz Allen consultant anywhere in the world, seeking to help a client with a particular problem, could now draw from the experience base of hundreds of colleagues. Editors "scrubbed" documents submitted to the system, clarifying questions and removing client-confidential material; there were incentives (both financial and in peer pressure) for even the busiest consultant to post relevant documents. Much of Knowledge OnLine's contents ultimately were repackaged for in-house training courses. A Harvard Business School case study reported that about 70 percent of Booz Allen's professionals used Knowledge OnLine at least once per month—a remarkably high usage rate for a system of this kind in the 1990s.

As WCB went through its transition, the Worldwide Technology Business faced a similar challenge. Its four separate technology organizations had begun to duplicate efforts and, while the business was still growing, it was not keeping pace with growth in public-sector consulting in general.

In 1993, seeing the impact that the V2K process was having on WCB, Bill Stasior urged WTB management to embark on a similar course of self-examination and renewal. Gary Mather, then WTB president, led the initial process, pairing up members of the WTB leadership team with other partners to conduct a diagnostic phase. By mid-1994, the result

was a series of task groups that were to reconsider both the culture and the structure of the government business. This led to a "blueprinting" effort to design a new WTB, which ultimately led to a team structure focused on markets rather than individual clients, a measurement and reward system that supported teaming and collaboration, and a new set of business models and values all aimed at delivering results for clients. Instead of seeing themselves in divi-

OUR VISION

To be the absolute best management and technology consulting firm measured by the value that we deliver to our clients and by our spirit of partnership

Worldwide Technology Business Service Mission

WTB's mission is to serve government agencies, institutions, and corporations in targeted global markets to help them achieve their mission—by making their mission "our mission"	We seek to build long term relationships and offer the full range of the Firm's services to meet clients' needs from mission definition through operations support	Our role is to bring to bear superior understanding of the client's environment coupled with outstanding functional expertise in management, technology, and engineering disciplines to create tailored solutions to meet key client challenges	To every client, we commit the breadth of the Firm's professional talent and the depth of its accumulated learning and methods	Our performance is measured by the quality of our work and the success of our clients, and by our reputation for service, objectivity, integrity, and results

We Commit Ourselves To

- Superior work quality and results for our clients. We seek a partnership with our clients in the pursuit of their objectives
- A team environment in which we strive to achieve the best results for our clients, our staff, and the Firm
- Maintaining superior capability and making the best deployment of that capability on every assignment
- Growing and strengthening our institution
- Building and nurturing our staff and a new generation of Partners
- Innovation and thought leadership

We will embed a teamwork ethic throughout our organization, whereby decisions and actions are driven by what is good for our clients and the Firm, and where clients, contracts, staff, and intellectual capital belong to the Firm and are managed by empowered teams

sions and practices, WTB partners would now work in client-focused teams (for ongoing work) and "campaigns" (for new projects). V2K led to a streamlining of WTB services, eliminating some of the lower-end program-management assignments and focusing on more strategic activities further up the value chain.

V2K became an incubator for future leaders of the firm—many of the partners with key roles in the aspiration, diagnostic, and blueprinting phases of V2K went on to become senior partners. Similar to the effort in WCB, the V2K process also developed its own knowledge-sharing program called Exploring the Leadership Challenge, a course nearly all WTB senior associates have attended since its inception.

Giving the V2K process further impetus, Ralph Shrader became president of WTB in 1994. Shrader clearly set Booz Allen's vision for its public-sector business—"to be the best, not the biggest"—and he and his leadership team outlined and executed a strategy of "Quality Growth" as the means to get there. This involved growing the business in areas

The vision statement for Booz Allen's Worldwide Technology Business, signed by partners in 2000, is a thematic update of the ethics statement developed by Carl Hamilton.

reflections

"I joined Booz Allen in Germany. I was in Berlin the night the wall came down. Now I live in the U.S., consulting with the Veteran's Administration on the system that processes disability checks. Guys who survived POW camps or the Bataan Death March write me, saying, 'Thank you so much; I now can afford chemo for my wife.'"

"I flew an A-6 Intruder bomber for 18 years, ending up in the U.S. Naval Strategic Command in Omaha. My daughter was in fifth grade then, and it was her fifth school district. I decided to retire from the military and got licensed to do home inspections, but then I got a call from Booz Allen Hamilton with an offer to open an office from my home."

"I worked in a Brazilian transportation company, importing a new line of truck tires from Japan. Then I went to Northwestern for an MBA. I was recruited by the Brazilian partners, who invited me to start a marketing department for the firm in Brazil."

"I got a PhD in experimental psychology. Then I founded a company to create a paperless record, but I couldn't line up the venture capital. Having a young family, I daddy-tracked myself instead and wrote a book on management before joining Booz Allen."

[**"There are a lot of people with interesting backgrounds: a pioneer in microfinance, a specialist in antique furniture, and a lot of former journalists."**]

"I had ten years in the nonprofit sector before I came here. I ran dance companies. There are a lot of people with interesting backgrounds: a pioneer in microfinance (making loans to rural community business people in developing countries), a specialist in antique furniture for an auction house, and a lot of former journalists."

"I grew up working summers on my uncle's farm. I decided I didn't want to be a farmer when I had to empty the silo in the middle of August. I started working overhauling nuclear submarines. Like the silo, it was too dirty, too dangerous, and too loud."

"I studied physics in Munich and worked with a Nobel Prize winner researching solar neutrinos. It was great, but I was reluctant to expose myself to radioactivity. Having pursued business studies during my PhD, I talked to Booz Allen. I think I signed the contract the same day I defended my thesis."

"I joined Booz Allen in the early 1980s. I read a book in 1989 called *A Walk Across America*. I resigned and bicycled around the U.S. for six months, then I went to England as part of my MBA program. I worked for a telecommunications company in the late 1990s. When the sector normalized, I rejoined Booz Allen."

"One of my passions is golf. I really didn't understand how important golf was until I came to Booz Allen."

"I played water polo for the German national team in the 1990 Olympics, but I didn't want to remain an athlete and do the same thing a second or third time. I chose a business career because of the team element; once again, I was with highly motivated colleagues who can work hard but also play hard."

At any moment, several thousand consultants, associates, and senior associates are on assignment for Booz Allen Hamilton. They are notable for the interesting lives they led before joining the firm and unique rewards they find in their present work. The above is just a sampling of their stories.

Leaders of a Booz Allen-assisted transformation at the U.S. Internal Revenue Service included, left to right, Chris Disher; Colleen Kelly, president of the National Treasury Employees Union; John Jones; Roger Blond; IRS Commissioner Charles Rossotti; Gary Mather; Ralph Shrader, chairman and CEO of Booz Allen; Gary Neilson; and John LaFaver, former IRS deputy commissioner for modernization.

in which the firm could deliver superior value to government clients, differentiate itself from competitors, and be profitable in this highly regulated business sector. Concurrently, Shrader launched a People Strategy within WTB to attract, develop, and reward the best people. A centerpiece of the People Strategy was the articulation of Booz Allen's ten Core Values, against which all employees are now measured (see page 127).

Partnership Prototypes: The IRS

In 1997 the U.S. Internal Revenue Service was beset with problems. The public ranked the agency among its least admired institutions. Congress responded in 1998, after a series of public hearings, by passing the IRS Restructuring and Reform Act, mandating that the agency "provide America's taxpayers top-quality service by helping them understand and meet their tax responsibilities and by applying the tax law with integrity and fairness to all."

The previous year, Charles Rossotti had become IRS commissioner after a 27-year-career in international business and information technology. He called upon Booz Allen to become the agency's partner for change. Over the next four years an extended Booz Allen team from both the commercial and government sides of the firm partnered with a team from all levels of the IRS. The goal: radically transform the agency from a 1950s-style, geographically structured matrix to a 21st-century, customer-focused enterprise.

With the advent of computer networks, low-cost phone and data service, and higher-quality information technology, it was no longer necessary to locate the nexus of service in the IRS's dozens of local offices (organized into 43 regional groups). "Technology shrank distances," says Rossotti, "and made it possible to create new forms of organization."

The project, led initially by Senior Vice Presidents Gary Mather and Gary Neilson, and Vice President John Jones, was the firm's first major use of a commercial-style strategic transformation with a government client. In 1998 and 1999 the reorganization put the IRS through the same kind of change Booz Allen had put itself through in the 1980s—a shift from regional to customer-focused leadership. Four operating divisions were established to serve the specific needs of different taxpayer groups: individuals with wage and investment income; the self-employed and small businesses; mid-size and large businesses; and tax-exempt and government businesses. The new system replaced a top-down decision-making process with a team approach in which a mix of people from different levels and with a diversity of skills focused on specific issues or projects. The agency also created new, shared services and placed a higher-than-ever emphasis on effectively answering taxpayers' questions and quickly expediting resolution of tax problems.

To be sure, there were hiccups as people adjusted to the new approach, but overall the results were impressive. Public confidence in the IRS rose 20 percent, and in one survey the agency was ranked as more friendly and efficient than many private-sector companies. Moreover, there was a dramatic rise in the IRS's collection rate. Underlying the effort, after all, was a theory that more customer-friendly tax-collection policies will not only make it easier for people to pay taxes, they will result in a less adversarial relationship that fosters compliance. The IRS and Booz Allen both won major awards for the effort: U.S. Vice President Al Gore's Council on Reinventing Government presented the IRS with its Hammer Award, and the IRS presented its Commissioner's Award to Booz Allen, which was the first external recipient in 20 years. Since then Booz Allen has used a commercial-government hybrid approach in other work: for example, at the United Kingdom's Department for Work and Pensions and at the U.S. Immigration and Naturalization Service.

Dot-Com Boom, Bubble, Bust

The Internet, which seemed to promise a fast track to unlimited riches, has been called the "overnight sensation that took 30 years to build." Late in the 1990s many businesses, including consulting firms, got caught in the euphoria as the World Wide Web fueled people's imaginations about new ways of connecting, sharing information, and doing business. They started virtual companies, bought the idea that they could ignore traditional business cycles, and sought to ride the wave of a "new economy" to new riches. Booz Allen established new practices to foster "e-business" and "Web-based sup-

The NASDAQ market, heavily weighted with technology stocks, endured the worst beating of the major exchanges in the dot-com bust of 2000.

ply chains." Some worried that, as the Internet transformed the supply chain, recruitment would suffer; management consulting, always a magnet for the best and brightest young business-school candidates, couldn't compete with the prospect of being a dot-com billionaire.

But Booz Allen's leaders were also explicitly circumspect. Many remembered the crisis of the 1970s, when they had gotten caught up in another business bubble and ultimately had to face the painful experience of raising the money to buy back their own firm. "We were very clear," said Vice President Klaus-Peter Gushurst, "that we

weren't going to let that happen again." They also recognized the limitations of e-commerce and Web-based business; thus, Booz Allen's consultations focused primarily on helping clients with established brick-and-mortar operations build a sustained and viable online presence. Among the firm's published notes of caution was a survey of "delivery density," showing that the business models for early online grocers, convenience stores, and generalized delivery services such as Webvan, Kozmo, and Urbanfetch couldn't sustain themselves. This stand was as unpopular in 1999 as Booz Allen's skepticism about the supersonic transport (SST) had been in the late 1960s.

Then, in April 2000, the bubble burst. Billions of dollars in market capitalization vanished, and within about 18 months hundreds of businesses—including Webvan and Kozmo (Urbanfetch reshaped itself as a more conventional delivery service)—went under. Booz Allen, like all the major consulting firms, was affected by the downturn. But unlike some other professional services competitors, the firm never sustained heavy losses from having overextended itself in the "e-hype." Many projects that other firms might have eliminated in lean times continued without interruption. The crash was painful, but it left the firm poised for change and challenge.

Transcending Boundaries

Booz Allen entered the new century with a new chairman and CEO—Ralph Shrader, whom the partners had elected in late 1998 in anticipation of the 1999 retirement of Bill Stasior. Shrader had spent his career in both the public and private sectors. He had joined Booz Allen in 1974 as an engineer specializing in computer communications and quickly rose through the management ranks. Shrader's personal consulting practice focused on the global telecommunications industry, and his experience on complex projects such as the divestiture of AT&T, the evolution of the U.S. Defense Department's National Communications System in the 1980s, and work for the U.N.'s International Telecommunications Union in Geneva reinforced his belief in the importance of bridging boundaries—organizational and geographic, to be sure, but also the invisible boundaries created by unspoken attitudes, assumptions, and cultural differences.

nder Shrader's leadership, Booz Allen grew strongly—nearly doubling in revenue between 1999 and 2004—but more significantly, the firm vaulted in external recognition and internal pride as the consultant of choice, employer of choice, and respected corporate citizen. Booz Allen increasingly took on the world's toughest problems, problems that required bridging public and private concerns—in national and international security, healthcare, global transportation, and the like. The firm's work and innovative ideas—about strategic and organizational leadership, CEO turnover, technology trends, and defense—were prominently featured in the global press on a daily basis. Booz Allen's higher profile was mirrored by top management, with Shrader becoming the firm's most visible modern chairman—regularly speaking at venues like the World Economic Forum, the Strategic Management Society, the Women's Center, and at the world's top business schools. Internally, the ten Core Values became an individual and institutional commitment for all, and People Survey results in both the Worldwide Technology Business and Worldwide Commercial Business showed employee pride and satisfaction at an all-time high.

By 2000 Booz Allen was doing more than just solving clients' problems. It was thinking strategically with them about boundary-breaking capabilities for their long-term development, and helping them weather unexpected storms in an environ-

Ralph Shrader, who took office as chairman and CEO of Booz Allen in 1999, has presided over a new set of strategic directions for the company.

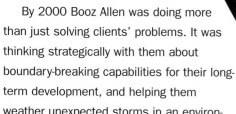

ment of change, uncertainty, and mutual dependency. It had become clearer than ever that ours is not only a pluralistic society, but a pluralistic world in which governments, corporations, nongovernmental organizations, and voluntary associations all interact in crucially interdependent but unpredictable and often unofficial ways. As countries around the world have learned, public buildings, private companies, communication networks, the power grid, public transit, sea lanes, food sources, and wilderness areas are all interconnected and susceptible to unpredictable forces—good and bad, from within and without.

In the wake of the bursting of the economic bubble in 2000, the reverberating effects of terrorist attacks around the world, corporate governance crises in the U.S. and in Europe, and audit reforms embedded in the Sarbanes-Oxley Act in the United States and similar legislation elsewhere, the management consulting business underwent an irreversible structural shift. The old prevailing business models for the profession were no longer viable. In both commercial- and public-sector consulting, much of the traditional work became commoditized— divided, repackaged, and outsourced to low-cost suppliers. As a result, consulting firms no longer have a monopoly on the brightest MBAs or the most advanced technological research. No consulting firm can expect high fees for standard-grade strategic work or merely mechanically adept implementation. Among the most pressing reasons that clients in the public and private sectors need consultants today is to help them quickly and effectively reorient their operations and management priorities in unison, in a way that links them comprehensively with customers and partners to produce enduring results.

To provide this kind of help, management consulting firms must continually stay one step ahead of not just competitors but clients—and themselves. Booz Allen has had to continually undergo the same kinds of visionary self-examination and transformation that it recommends to clients.

Strategy-Based Transformation

As the new century began, Booz Allen took stock of its position in the market, assessing the need for its own strategic transformation. Over the course of six months, it interviewed its partners and their clients, comparing the firm's vision, its capabilities, and the aspirations of its partners with the needs and aspirations of its clients.

Booz Allen's leaders realized that the firm's evolution had created a unique strength—an ability to integrate multifunctional capabilities with specialized understanding of commercial industries and government sectors to meet the individual needs of every client. Reinforcing this was

a team structure in which commercial and public-sector consultants alike could flexibly adopt, for the sake of a client, the practices and organizational approaches of the other—and they could use Booz Allen's firmwide intranet and other knowledge-sharing and collaboration tools to leverage the firm's cumulative experience and facilitate the rapid exchange of ideas. Together, these capabilities added up to a critical source of competitive differentiation and a valued service that Booz Allen could offer every client: the full expertise and experience of the firm.

Meanwhile, out of the firm's experience with clients and in-depth studies of some of its most successful consultations emerged the concept of strategy-based transformation (SBT). Driven by Dan Lewis, president of

Dennis Doughty, left, and Dan Lewis, right, are presidents of Booz Allen's two operating units, the Worldwide Technology Business and Worldwide Commercial Business, respectively. Their consulting teams frequently collaborate to serve government and corporate clients.

In 2000 British Prime Minister Tony Blair announced his government's ambition to be "the world's best environment for e-commerce." To benchmark the country's readiness and capability as an "e-economy" hub, Booz Allen has worked with the U.K. government's Office of the e-Envoy, the INSEAD business school, and the Information Age Partnership.

the Worldwide Commercial Business, SBT seeks to make a client resilient so that any changes implemented in its organization or operations don't just overcome an immediate, narrowly defined problem; they boost the organization's capacity to meet challenges continually. Moreover, the changes are intrinsically tied to the organization's core aspirations and direction.

As explained in *strategy+business*, a publication of Booz Allen, "A strategy-based transformation is an opportunity to make a significant change and lasting improvement in the value of [an organization] by taking it in a new direction using any number of different approaches—mergers, restructurings, new business models, new markets, or a combination thereof." Corporations and governments must now expect that, at any moment, they will be confronted with market challenges, risks, and even calamities: organizational misalignments, changing competitive environments, infrastructure failures, computer viruses, currency fluctuations, economic jolts, and various forms of terrorism or political unrest. They are best handled as part of an overarching strategic approach in which adaptive decision making throughout an organization is linked directly to the design of business processes and information technology, and to the development of people. In most change initiatives, only one or two of these elements are typically covered, or they are all handled separately. Instead, Booz Allen suggests to clients that these domains of change need to be considered together—if not explicitly, then implicitly. One early example was Booz Allen's

work to support Nissan CEO Carlos Ghosn in his firm's efforts to design a new global organizational framework and operating model to sustain better performance on an ongoing basis.

This view was grounded directly in Booz Allen's own experience. Vision-driven reorganizations in each of the firm's major units, the Worldwide Commercial Business (WCB) and the Worldwide Technology Business (WTB), had shown how seemingly intractable institutional paralysis could be overcome— and revealed the power released when organizational silos are broken down. Shrader points to healthcare as one of several cases that demonstrate the value of such cross-functional solutions. "WTB works with the federal government health agencies— the FDA, for example—on drug approvals and safety. So for the pharmaceutical companies who come to WCB, our knowledge of the regulatory regime is extremely helpful. When our two groups found each other and began working together, they could look at the whole system as if starting from scratch: How would you organize our practice to improve the broad healthcare market? And what kinds of beneficial changes are possible by leveraging change on both sides?"

Combined teams from WCB and WTB also have collaborated on projects for the Internal Revenue Service and Washington, D.C., police department in the United States, and the Department for Work and Pensions (DWP) in the United Kingdom. They have been among the most successful engagements in Booz Allen's history. Clearly, Booz Allen has experienced many of the same victories and tensions as its clients, and is in a unique position to help them deal with this era of transformational change.

Against this backdrop, Booz Allen changed its name for the first time in 60 years as part of a major brand-building initiative led by Shrader. It removed the bullet and ampersand from Booz•Allen & Hamilton's corporate and subsidiary names and adopted the global brand name, Booz Allen Hamilton. More important, it embraced a single business definition for the entire firm ("global strategy and technology consulting firm"), a new, one-phrase mission ("Booz Allen Hamilton works with clients to deliver results that endure"), and bold new graphics to communicate its shared vision and distinctive model of cross-boundary collaboration. While Booz Allen still is divided into two divisions, each with its own operating model and compensation structure, the firm's partners and employees recognize that their future lies together—Booz Allen will solve public- and private-sector client problems without regard for whether the solution fits a commercial or government business model. It will help governments adopt the high-performance mindset and fast-paced strategic decision making of commercial enterprise; and it will help business master the intricate ethical and technological demands of infrastructure maintenance, risk management, corporate governance, and public presence. "We're looking ahead," says Senior Vice President Samuel Strickland, "to a world in which the distinction between commercial business and government business is less important than it was."

Among the sectors where Booz Allen can apply its cross-boundary thinking and capabilities is the troubled airline industry, which transcends business and government on a global scale. The firm's consultants have been attuned to the industry for years, in part because of a mid-1990s initiative that reorganized a leading airplane manufacturer around lean manufacturing and better aircraft design. No improvement by a single manufacturer, however, could resolve a systemic problem facing the entire industry: a business model that no longer serves manufacturers, carriers, or their customers.

As Dan Lewis notes, the longstanding hub-and-spoke system was based on the economic logic of railroad terminals: central switching was more cost-effective than point-to-point travel. But as multiple airlines competed through multiple hubs, overcapacity

Three Booz Allen employees lost their lives in service to their country when terrorists attacked the Pentagon on 9/11. The attacks revealed the importance of cross-boundary communication and collaboration—an expertise Booz Allen had been developing in the 1990s. Vice President Lloyd Howell, right, lights a candle at a memorial for his former colleagues while, above, twin light towers point skyward in a 2002 commemoration at Ground Zero in New York.

Since the 1980s Booz Allen has expanded its global presence along with the diversity of its workforce. Germany, as symbolized by Berlin's Brandenburg Gate, above, has been among the firm's most vital European markets. The Diversity Award, right, has been one of Booz Allen's most prestigious honors given to individual employees and teams since 1999.

befell the industry. Southwest Airlines adopted a different approach and revealed the underlying inefficiencies of the hub-and-spoke system—transferring bags and people, coordinating schedules, and handling missed connections added complexity and cost. "Except for international hubs," says Lewis, "the existing system is doomed."

The nature of air travel is an evolving target; it's still not clear exactly what the typical flight of, say, 2014 will look like, especially with the extant threat of terrorism. But there is already one visible sign: even stodgy airlines are willing to experiment. They know, in part from watching low-cost airlines make money during tough times that left many of them in or verging on bankruptcy, that their survival depends on it.

Response, Recovery, and Resilience

On September 11, 2001, terrorists crashed airplanes into New York's World Trade Center and the Pentagon in Washington, D.C., and brought down another over a field in Pennsylvania—exposing a once-unfathomable American vulnerability as well as dangerous flaws in cross-organizational information sharing, communication, and collaboration. Moreover, the attacks revealed just how comprehensive a security infrastructure would be needed to protect the world against terrorism, and how complex it would be to create and maintain such a system.

Shrader and other top Booz Allen executives were in a midtown New York hotel on the morning of 9/11, attending a meeting of

the WCB's partners. Like many other people stranded after the collapse of the trade-center towers, they tried frantically to contact their families to tell them they were OK. In Washington, however, not everyone was as fortunate. Three Booz Allen employees—Gerald P. Fisher, Terence M. Lynch, and Ernest M. Willcher—died when American Airlines Flight 77 hit the Pentagon; they had been meeting with U.S. Army Lieutenant General Timothy J. Maude, discussing a Web-based tool for handling survivors' benefits. On the day of September 11, of course, no one knew how many people might be lost. Throughout Booz Allen's offices, people scrambled to confirm the whereabouts and safety of employees—while others fanned out through the nation's capital, helping clients ranging from the Department of Defense to the Federal Bureau of Investigation. Everyone knew this would change the nature of their work and their world for a long time to come.

Events since 9/11—wars in Afghanistan and Iraq; terrorist attacks in Bali, Saudi Arabia, and Madrid; political change in Africa, Asia, and South America; ethical scandals and governance crises in some American and European corporations; and the changing geopolitical and economic roles of China, Japan, the United Kingdom, and the United States—have underlined the essential uncertainties of our time. Moreover, they have underscored the importance of Booz Allen's notion of resilience—that an organization's success depends on its ability to transform itself in the face of continuous change while maintaining the core values that have allowed it to endure. "Resilience" may have sounded abstract before September 11, but it rapidly became an extremely practical concept.

Booz Allen has developed a number of tools for promoting enterprise resilience. They include diagnostics of risk strategy, computer-based "war games" that help companies rehearse their response to crises before they happen, and blueprints for corporate organizational forms that foster endurance and success, even in the face of advanced risk.

The Best Ideas

To a management historian, consulting firms (including Booz Allen) have traditionally played a dual role in the world of ideas. Their teams, sometimes deliberately and sometimes inadvertently, have gathered the in-depth empirical data on which management thinking is based. And they have excelled at taking management theories and testing them in the mercurial and imperfect, but unavoidable, laboratories of real-world organizations. Yet with a very few exceptions, management consultants tended not to be theorists. Academics theorized; consultants disseminated and practiced.

Or so it went in the past. Since the late 1990s, Booz Allen has changed its approach, making a deliberate attempt to instill management theory—and the building of theories—in all aspects of its practice and with all of its consultants, not just a few "stars."

For instance, the idea and application of "smart customization" is at the heart of a

Booz Allen's Düsseldorf office, above, which celebrates its 40th anniversary in 2005, has long been a creative hub. Left, the Southern Cone region (Brazil, Argentina, and Chile) honored the firm's 90th anniversary with a watery staff meeting.

Innovations in Thought Leadership

Booz Allen Hamilton has a long history of publishing groundbreaking thought leadership that makes a difference for business and government. The firm's emphasis on developing and sharing knowledge goes back to its roots. In the 1940s, Ed Booz wrote a set of guidelines for living well. Although it went unpublished officially, it started a tradition of authorship in which Booz Allen people have communicated their ideas, insights, and passions across a variety of media. The firm's global presence and the cross-sector nature of its work contribute to the depth and breadth of its thought leadership.

At the forefront of its thinking is *strategy+business*, the award-winning quarterly journal Booz Allen launched in 1995. The magazine publishes articles written by such leading management luminaries as C. K. Pralahad and Nobel-prize-winning economist Daniel Kahneman, who share the pages with Booz Allen's own consultants and other in-house business innovators. Bridging the gap between theory and practice, pioneering yet practicable ideas appear on topics that include corporate governance, innovation, change management, supply chain management, and strategy-based transformation. Appearing annually in *s+b* is Booz

Allen's study of CEO turnover at the world's 2,500 largest publicly traded companies. The report, first conducted in 2001, has become the benchmark reference for business leaders and is quoted widely in the world press.

Introduced in 2003, *s+b* "Readers" are

Published since 1995, *strategy+business* has become a leading business and management magazine and a flagship vehicle for thought leaders from within and outside the firm.

book-sized collections of the firm's best ideas on critical business and management topics. Titles include *Enterprise Resilience: Risk and Security in the Networked World*, *Making Overhead Outperform: Next-Generation G&A Performance*, and the two-volume set devoted to strategy-based transformation, *The Case for Transformation* and *Transformation Cases*. In 2004, *strategy+business* and Booz Allen teamed with the European Executive Council to publish *CEO: Chief European Officer—Business Leadership in Europe*, thoughtful essays by 20 CEOs and senior executives running the European operations of some of the world's largest multinationals.

The firm's most powerful concepts, including how to analyze a company's organizational DNA and how healthcare issues affect both the public and private sectors, have appeared in the world's leading business and trade periodicals as well as in its own intellectual capital, or white papers. Booz Allen devotes substantial effort to surveying executives to gauge their thoughts on current business issues. The "Do Values Create Value?" survey, first undertaken in Europe in 2003, has led to a series of values-related initiatives, including *Werte schaffen Wert* (*Values Create Value: Why We Need*

Trustworthy Executives), by Munich-based vice presidents Gregor Vogelsang and Christian Burger.

In the recent past, Booz Allen partners and other staff members have published an assortment of books, among them *The Trillion-Dollar Enterprise: How the Alliance Revolution Will Transform Global Business*, by former Senior Vice President Cyrus Freidheim; *Channel Champions: How Leading Companies Build New Strategies to Serve Customers*, by Senior Vice President Steven Wheeler and Vice President Evan Hirsh; and *Creative Destruction: Business Survival Strategies in the Global Internet Economy*, by Vice President Raul Katz and Paul Vaaler.

The firm's international presence and perspective means that its thought leadership appears across the globe in a variety of languages, in such books as *Faktor Menschlichkeit* (*The Human Factor: Management Culture in a Changing World*), by Munich-based Senior Vice President Rolf Habbel; *Building a 100 Year Company: Finding the Way Towards Sustained Performance*, by Tokyo-based Vice President Junichi Handa; and *Next TV: La via italiana al digitale terrestre* (*Next TV: The Italian Way to Digital Terrestrial TV*), by Milan-based Vice President Luigi Pugliese.

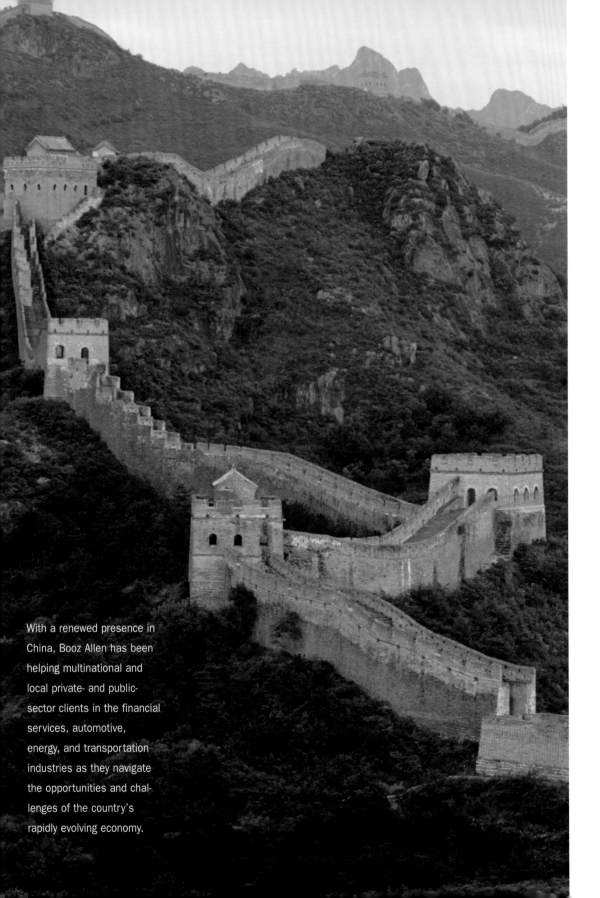

With a renewed presence in China, Booz Allen has been helping multinational and local private- and public-sector clients in the financial services, automotive, energy, and transportation industries as they navigate the opportunities and challenges of the country's rapidly evolving economy.

Booz Allen theory of cost effectiveness: making many products for many customers doesn't have to add costs. It does mean added complexity, which typically boosts expense, but those who learn to distinguish value-added complexity (where customers embrace many products) from gratuitous complexity (where customers basically don't care) can outpace competitors dramatically. Studies by the firm have found striking performance gains among "smart customizers"—managers who have learned how to discern when the additional complexity is worthwhile and have reshaped their production processes accordingly. The firm has found that companies that are "smart customizers" tend to outperform industry peers two-to-one in revenue growth and have profit margins 5 percent to 10 percent above those of their competitors.

Booz Allen's work on intrinsic innovation effectiveness takes a similarly tailored approach. In this theory of innovation, some products and processes demand in-depth investment in production innovation, others demand breakthroughs only in marketing, and others do better with a minimum of any kind of innovation. The trick to being successful lies in knowing which products require

Nations will become even more interdependent: No country will be able to confront terrorism or environmental and health problems alone.

what types of innovation at what times in their life cycles. Being able to diagnose this can be the remedy for a perennial, and tragic, story—companies that bet their futures on innovation but can't translate their new investments into revenue or profitability.

Underlying all of this work is a recognition that every organization's success depends on its ability to effectively execute a strategy attuned to its own unique nature. Recently, Booz Allen developed a model to help companies identify their organizational DNA, which starts with the premise that there are four basic building blocks of organizational character: decision rights (explicit and implicit policies that determine who is accountable for which results), information flows (including key metrics), motivators (objectives, incentives, and career patterns), and structure (the design of the hierarchy). Combined, these tend to produce recurring organizational "species," each with its own qualities and distinctive ways of responding to customers and interveners: Military, Resilient, Just-in-Time, Over-managed, Fits-and-Starts, Outgrown, and Passive-Aggressive. An online survey developed by Booz Allen allows people to quickly assess their own companies' DNA by answering questions about the

behaviors and patterns they observe—and to specify the remedies that would help produce organizational transformation.

International Presence

In the aftermath of the currency crises of the 1990s and the shock of September 11, 2001, Booz Allen's international business went through a retrenchment, particularly in Latin America and Asia. Some offices could not survive; others languished; and those which flourished, like the offices in Western Europe, depended on a vibrant and active partnership team. The firm's GSA group, for example, which represents Germany, Switzerland, and Austria, is one of the strongest parts of the firm, with profitable and growing businesses in both the private and public sectors.

Despite the challenges, Booz Allen's commitment to a global presence is stronger than it has ever been, with more than 100 offices on six continents. The firm is investing seriously in several parts of the world where it has never quite managed to gain a permanent footing in the past. In Tokyo, Booz Allen recently acquired Gemini Consulting Japan, doubling the staff in Asia

Booz Allen consultants worked with the Saudi Telecom Company as it undertook a four-year privatization effort. Since 2000 Booz Allen has worked on a strategy-based transformation at Thailand's Bangkok Bank. The Thai unit of currency is the baht, top left.

The annual U.S. Marine Corps Reserve Toys for Tots campaign is just one of the many community charities Booz Allen supports. Above, Chairman and CEO Ralph Shrader gets into the giving spirit.

Aeronáutica, explore innovative financing. Australia and New Zealand are also sites of renewed activity.

Booz Allen has been present in the Middle East since the mid-1950s, serving a wide variety of government and commercial clients, including the Saudi Telecom Company, the governments of the UAE and Jordan, as well as a number of industrial and financial services companies. Booz Allen is also active on social and pro bono initiatives, including "universal internet access" strategies in the Gulf countries and an automobile-safety program in Lebanon, established by Booz Allen senior consultant Youssef Heneine after a former classmate was killed in a traffic accident.

In the United Kingdom, Booz Allen is helping the Department for Work and Pensions conduct a reorganization similar in scope and impact to the revamping of the U.S. Internal Revenue Service in the late 1990s. The DWP is the largest civil service entity in Great Britain; it annually disburses billons of pounds in pensions, unemployment and disability benefits, and child-support payments. "Retirees looking for information about their pensions," says London-based Vice President Shumeet Banerji, "will be the real ones to benefit from our work." Booz Allen also continues to support a U.K. government initiative to benchmark the country's e-commerce progress annually against other leading economies and to identify ways to help its citizens, businesses, and government agencies make more and better use of information and communications technology. This work is an example of how Booz Allen

and business in the region. Offices have opened in Shanghai, Singapore, and Thailand. One notable client is Bangkok Bank, whose CEO, Chartsiri Sophonpanich, asked Booz Allen to help him revitalize his organization and thus retain its preeminent standing in the Thai marketplace.

There is also a Latin American resurgence, led by São Paulo-based Vice President Leticia Costa—the first woman to head a Booz Allen office. Among the projects she has championed are a study on internationalizing Brazilian companies and a pro bono project to help one of Brazil's top engineering colleges, the Instituto Tecnológico de

Harlem Small Business Initiative

One of the most comprehensive pro bono projects in which Booz Allen has participated is the Harlem Small Business Initiative, co-organized with the William J. Clinton Presidential Foundation, New York University's Stern School of Business, and the National Black MBA Association. Since 2002 consultants from Booz Allen have provided technical support to entrepreneurs with vibrant businesses but without the training or knowledge required to grow them. The Harlem-based businesses—in a New York community experiencing a spurt of economic growth amid many economic challenges—have included a hat shop, a restaurant, a dentist, and a plumber. The plumber, for example, had run his business for 40 years without an income statement or a balance sheet. The initiative tested Booz Allen's imagination as well as its ability to impart knowledge, since the support the firm provided needed to be implemented by people with no business-school training.

Senior Vice President Reggie Van Lee, who organized Booz Allen's participation, has a long history of involvement in community work and the arts. A former professional dancer with the Alvin Ailey American Dance Theater and board member of the Dance Theatre of Harlem, Van Lee helped organize the latter's groundbreaking tour of

In December 2002, former U.S. President Bill Clinton spoke in the New York offices of Booz Allen about the Harlem Small Business Initiative. Pictured above, from left to right, are Booz Allen Senior Vice President Reggie Van Lee; Clyde Williams, domestic policy advisor to Clinton; Lynne Fairbanks; and Booz Allen Vice President David Knott. Pictured right, Clinton and Van Lee.

the Soviet Union in the late 1980s. He is currently a trustee and treasurer of the Studio Museum in Harlem.

For the Small Business Initiative, Van Lee, who has an engineering degree from MIT and a Harvard MBA, was adamant that Booz Allen's participants in the program make a wholehearted and long-term commitment from the beginning. "If people wanted to make a real difference, they would have to find time for it in evenings or weekends," Van Lee says. "I sent an e-mail around the New York office explaining this and 80 people showed up at the initial meeting. That was in 2002; and 70 percent of the people who

signed up stuck with it for two years. The businesses involved have doubled revenues and increased profitability. The business owners embraced the staff and saw them as part of their families."

One of the Harlem entrepreneurs told Van Lee, "These Booz Allen kids are dedicating all this time. They're not getting any money for it. How dare I not get excited about moving my business ahead when they're so excited?'"

In May 2004 the Clinton Foundation announced that it was expanding the initiative into the New York City boroughs of Brooklyn and the Bronx.

Booz Allen helped the United States Transportation Command (TRANSCOM)—whose communication room is shown above—develop TRAC2ES, a Web-based system that tracks and coordinates the movement of sick and injured service-men and women.

has worked with other European public sectors, such as in the Netherlands and Germany, to use the Internet more effectively in communications with citizens.

Europe, in the process of assimilating formerly communist Poland, the Czech Republic, Hungary, and the Baltic states, faces inevitable pressure, as Booz Allen Vice President Klaus-Peter Gushurst notes, "to become a more performance-driven society." The historic divide between capitalism and communism is being replaced with an effort to rethink the rules of capitalism. Though some consider that effort largely over, more likely it is actually just beginning as the European Union, China, India, and other

emerging giant capitalist economies seek ways to blend laissez-faire policies with quality-of-life protections. Nations will become even more interdependent; no country will be able to confront terrorism or environmental and health problems alone.

Games of War and Peace

Booz Allen's support to the military, a mainstay of the firm's work since World War II, continues to foster technologies and methodologies that can be applied elsewhere, such as in industry and civilian government. For example, in 1998 Booz Allen began working with the U.S. Department of Defense to redesign the process for providing medical treatment to sick or injured soldiers, their families, and veterans. Booz Allen helped the military create an information-driven system called TRAC2ES (pronounced "traces") that makes use of all available technology (including cargo planes, with their well-designed tracking systems) to speed those in need to an appropriate medical facility. As of mid-2004 TRAC2ES had tracked more than 14,000 patients. It will not be long before the kind of real-time, widespread information flow at the heart of TRAC2ES is the basis of healthcare and other public services around the world.

Booz Allen has also been involved in supporting the U.S. Department of Homeland Security, which united 180,000 people from 22 federal agencies (many state agencies participated, too) in service to a critical and extremely difficult mission: prevent attacks and disasters, and, in the event they do occur,

A colorful arch, left, with an international theme welcomed ticket holders to the 2004 Booz Allen Classic, a PGA Tour charity fund-raising event held at the Tournament Players Club at Avenel in Potomac, Maryland. Below, the short but challenging ninth hole.

"There are dozens of examples of Booz Allen's continuing corporate commitment to community service."

provide emergency relief and recovery. This is arguably the largest "post-merger integration" project ever conducted. Additionally, the new department has conducted a series of Booz Allen–led strategic simulations known as war games: collaborative problem-solving exercises that allow participants to work through in advance logistical issues involved in complex and fast-moving situations. Often these reveal blind spots and critical gaps before an emergency actually takes place.

Originally developed in the 1980s by Booz Allen Vice President Mark Herman and a team of game designers for the U.S. Department of Defense, war games have helped military leaders establish procedures for procurement, equipment maintenance, transportation, and other logistical details, as well as set priorities for missions, tactics, and doctrine. Since the 1990s, war games have also been used by corporations—a manufacturer mulling potential alliances, an energy provider deciding whether to make massive investments in new technologies, a utility forging a long-term strategy under deregulation, a telecommunications company entering the wireless market, a diesel-engine manufacturer anticipating the loss of key customers.

A typical war game takes place over several days in a multimedia-enhanced room. Several teams play the roles of organizations acting in the system—a military battalion or maybe a corporate business unit. Teams are separated from one another and communicate only through e-mail; thus they are as isolated from their counterparts in

Booz Allen Hamilton's 90th-anniversary celebrations featured a U.S. Western Region climb up Pike's Peak in Colorado, above, and, right, a birthday party at the Booz Allen Hamilton Family Center in McLean, Virginia.

the system as they typically would be in the real world. The game, like life, throws challenges at its participants—hostile takeover attempts, military coups, tornadoes. In each round of play, teams make their moves and then, through maps, diagrams, statistical displays, and stories, see the impact of their decisions on the game's environment and on the other players. Participants can play the game over and over, make different decisions, and compare the impact. In debriefing sessions after the games, players talk through the choices they made, the reasoning underlying those choices, and the lessons they learned.

War games are proving invaluable at bringing diverse constituents together to forge the mutual understanding required to resolve complex issues. Senior Vice President Mark Gerencser has utilized war games as a key element of the firm's enterprise resilience work. One such war game, which brought together U.S. federal and local government and private-sector participants, focused on assessing the vulnerability of America's ports, cargo transportation system, and supply chains. Another game, co-sponsored with the Business Roundtable, an association of CEOs of leading corporations, simulated cyber-terrorist attacks on the accounting systems of two major banks combined with a plague outbreak. In yet another war game—co-sponsored by the nonprofit Council for Excellence in Government—75 public- and private-sector healthcare professionals explored the potential effects of a bioterrorism attack. All of these games have highlighted the need for a new kind of public-

reflections

Imagine that you have just graduated from a top business school, a leading university with a technical degree, or that you've distinguished yourself in business or government and want to enter the consulting profession. You would now be ripe for recruitment into Booz Allen Hamilton, but perhaps not if intellectual achievement is the only thing on your résumé. In the words of Senior Vice President David Newkirk, "We look for someone who has done something very hard, and very well—like run in a marathon, or climbed a mountain, or sung in an opera."

Among those serving clients of Booz Allen are former journalists, military officers and government officials, professional and ranking amateur athletes, inventors, and veterans of corporate innovation, academia, and entrepreneurial start-ups. Depending on your background and seniority, you may enter the professional ranks at any level. Throughout all stages of your career, you would work as part of a team. Inevitably, you would develop talents and experience in a particular area, focused either in an industry or domain, or in a functional specialty.

A senior associate articulates this way of looking at the arc of career growth: "It's all about people develop-

ment. You start by developing your own skills, and then the skills of the clients you're working with on assignments. At the senior professional levels, you're developing the skills of other Booz Allen people. At the highest levels—partner or senior partner—you're developing the capability of the most senior leadership, the CEOs and other top officials—and the entire organizations they work for. All three areas—developing yourself, your colleagues, and your clients—support one another; the better you get at one, the better you get at all of them."

The same spirit of commitment, particularly on behalf of clients, exists at every level of the firm. "When I describe what extraordinary things the support staff do at Booz Allen," Senior Vice President Gerald Adolph says, "people from other companies are astonished. An assistant or staff member will go out of their way to make sure that a report is done or that a client gets a package on a Saturday night. If you ask someone at Booz Allen, 'Who's your boss?' they might be confused—they might tell you what team or function they're in. But if you ask, 'Who's your client?' you get an immediate answer."

Leadership and client service has been the heart of the work, in a very real sense, since the days of Edwin G. Booz.

Heather Burns, a Booz Allen senior vice president, was one of the first women in the firm's public-sector business. Hired in the 1970s for her environmental expertise, Burns recalls, "If you delivered creativity and dedication to the job, you didn't have to fit a certain mold." She currently co-leads the firm's global healthcare business.

private partnership in the pursuit of homeland security.

As war games evolve and find new application, they could well change the nature of collective decision making far from battlefields or corporate boardrooms—and with powerful implications for the health or even survival of humankind. In early 2004 Booz Allen conducted a war-game simulation of HIV/AIDS in India. Conducted over two days for the Global Business Coalition on HIV/AIDS, the exercise involved an array of organizations including local governments, pharmaceutical companies, religious foundations, and the United Nations. The stakes of the real-world problem are high. If, as in parts of Africa, HIV/AIDS in India were to reach a 35 percent incidence rate, 350 million people could be affected. Collaborative solutions clearly will be needed, regardless of the ultimate magnitude of the crisis.

As Booz Allen Senior Vice President Heather Burns recalls from the HIV/AIDS simulation, "Most people came expecting a conference. Instead, they were thrown together to work on these specific issues. They came up with amazing ways to do things together. For instance, there were negotiations between the government and pharmaceutical companies to eliminate some drug tariffs in exchange for lower prices. Industrial facilities agreed with local communities to provide in-kind services, such as the use of their training facilities and clinics. People left with specific things they wanted to do; and for the first time, they could see each other through the other person's eyes."

Enduring Values, Enduring Results

Booz Allen has been recognized for its results and its policies by organizations worldwide. Recently:

- Kennedy Information's 2003 study, *The Client-Side Intelligence Report: Purchasing Behavior, Brand Awareness & Firm Perceptions*, ranked Booz Allen No. 1 in perception and performance among general management consulting firms in the United States;
- The Professional Services Council, the Fairfax County Chamber of Commerce, and *Washington Technology* magazine named Booz Allen the 2003 Government Contractor of the Year;
- *Washingtonian, Working Mother*, and The Netherlands' *Het Financieele Dagblad* published articles citing Booz Allen among the world's best places to work.

These and other honors demonstrate that Booz Allen is not only brains—it's also heart. There are dozens of examples of Booz Allen's continuing corporate commitment to community service. In 2004 the firm set a goal to raise $1 million per year over three years to charities in the Washington, D.C., area—through the Booz Allen Classic, the PGA Tour golf tournament for which the firm signed on as title sponsor beginning in 2004. Shrader saw the Booz Allen Classic as another way to strengthen the firm's spirit of service and brand recognition, and he led the process to gain inter-

Professional Excellence Awards

Started in 1986, the Booz Allen Hamilton Professional Excellence Awards (PEA) represent the firm's highest level of professional recognition. As Senior Vice President Heather Burns, chairperson of the award committee in 2004, puts it, "Each of these assignments represents the best of what Booz Allen can accomplish in partnership with our clients." Each year a committee of partners (often winners of previous awards) picks between two and five winners from nominees around the world, using a set of criteria tied to Booz Allen's mission of delivering enduring results: high-impact work, excellent performance and results, incisive thinking, and the ability to work with clients to meet both immediate and long-term goals in an ongoing relationship. Many of the stories in this book, since 1986 at least, involve PEA winners.

- It is always better to tell the truth, even at the risk of losing a relationship or job;
- The answer to a problem is never just technical; the human factor always makes a critical difference;
- No matter how big or small Booz Allen may get, the point is not to be the biggest, or even the most profitable, but the best.

In the end, a consulting firm has nothing but its people and their ideas to offer clients. Booz Allen's distinction may be simply the awareness that the same is true for every organization it works with: corporate or governmental, large or small, military or civilian, European or Asian or African or Australian or American, the long-term success of any enterprise depends on its ability to attract, develop, and deploy skilled people with great ideas. Ed Booz knew that in 1914.

Arguably, in the future, business and organizational leaders will come to recognize it too, until it becomes second nature: to increase the quality of results, increase the quality of people. Then the task of management consultants will be to learn, and to teach, the fine art of cultivating the best of human beings in an organizational setting. With ever more expansive thinking and an increasingly diverse workforce of people with world-changing ideas, Booz Allen Hamilton will continue to play the roles it has learned and practiced for 90 years—generator of knowledge about organizations and operations, broker between new and old ways, solver of complex problems, catalyst for change, and inventor of the future.

nal buy-in from the partners for the sponsorship and played a visible role as the tournament's external spokesperson.

Booz Allen also partners with the ePhilanthropy Foundation, advising nonprofit groups around the world on how to use the Internet for fund raising and relationship building; and it continues to contribute to charities chosen by employees. More than 500 Booz Allen staff members, along with family and friends, helped revitalize 29 homes in 18 U.S. cities in 2003 alone for a charity called Christmas in April, which renovates homes for low-income families with young children. Similar initiatives have taken place with the Australian office of Habitat for Humanity, the London-based Baron's Court project for the mentally ill, the Alnitak project for environmental clean-up of Lebanon's beaches, and many other places.

One could draw a direct line between these initiatives and Edwin G. Booz's original insight about people—that their quality, not the quality of technology or financial performance, represents the root cause of organizational success. That's the ultimate meaning, perhaps, of the Booz Allen corporate slogan: "Enduring values, enduring institutions, enduring results." Booz Allen's ability to serve, and to influence the world, depends entirely on the way in which the people of the firm live up to its values:

Timeline

The U.S. Navy, whose destroyer escorts freighters in World War II's Battle of the Atlantic, became a key Booz Allen client in 1940.

1910s

1914
Edwin G. Booz graduates with a master's degree from Northwestern University and establishes The Business Research Service, a consulting firm headquartered in the Otis Building in Chicago. His first major client is the Illinois State Railroad.

1917
Drafted into the U.S. Army, Booz works for the Army's personnel system during World War I.

1919
Booz returns to Chicago and names his company Business Engineering Service. Early clients include the State Bank & Trust Company of Evanston, Illinois.

Ed Booz produced this promotional brochure for his firm in 1926.

1920s

1924
The firm changes its name to Edwin G. Booz Surveys.

1925
George W. Fry joins the firm.

1929
James L. Allen joins the firm as it moves to the new Chicago Daily News Building. Major clients include U.S. Gypsum Company, Goodyear Tire & Rubber Co., Montgomery Ward, the Chicago Daily News, and the Chicago Tribune.

1930s

1934
Allen leaves the firm to take a position at Ditto, Inc.

The firm opens its first branch office, in New York City, with Fry in charge.

1935
The firm changes its name to Edwin G. Booz and Fry Surveys.

Carl L. Hamilton, from Weyerhaeuser, joins as partner.

1936
Allen returns and the firm becomes a four-person partnership called Booz, Fry, Allen and Hamilton.

1940s

1940
Hired by incoming Secretary of the Navy Frank Knox, the firm begins its long relationship with the U.S. Navy, helping it gear up for World War II.

1942-43
Booz and Fry dispute the future of government consulting. Allen temporarily leaves the firm and Fry resigns to start his own consulting business. Allen later returns and the firm adopts the name Booz, Allen & Hamilton.

An Allied war poster from early in World War II.

Booz Allen families met at the home of partner John Burns for the midyear partner party in 1950.

1950s

1960s

1944
Fortune magazine features Booz Allen in a lengthy article about management consulting headlined, "The Doctors of Management."

1945
A long phase of fast growth begins; there are now eight partners, 129 staff members, and offices in Chicago, New York, and Los Angeles. Other offices soon follow in Minneapolis, Washington, and San Francisco.

1946
Hamilton dies of a heart attack. Booz semi-retires; Allen becomes the partner in charge of the firm.

1947
Staff exceeds 100. Sales exceed $2 million.

1950s
Postwar expansion brings numerous clients, including Johnson Wax, RCA, NBC, and Cessna.

1951
Booz dies following a stroke.

1953
First major project outside the United States (a land-ownership study for the government of the Philippines).

1955
The firm creates a new subsidiary, Booz Allen Applied Research (BAAR-INC), forerunner of today's Worldwide Technology Business, for technical consulting and government contracting.

1956
The firm creates its Booz Allen & Hamilton International subsidiary.

1957
Booz Allen opens an office in Zurich, its first outside the United States.

Two critical pieces of the firm's intellectual property are developed, the "product life cycle" and the "critical path" (or PERT) process.

1958
Staff exceeds 300. Sales reach $7 million.

1961
Charles P. Bowen is appointed president of Booz, Allen & Hamilton.

1962
Booz Allen changes its structure from a partnership to a privately held corporation.

1969
Sales reach $55 million, having doubled since 1956.

Ed Booz led partners' wives in a dance to "My Little Grass Shack" in 1951. Betsy Pocock headed the line, while Minna Emch played piano.

Booz Allen published *Outlook*, a respected management magazine, beginning in 1980.

Booz Allen moved into a new building in McLean, Virginia, in 1992. Seen in a recent photograph, the site is now a five-building campus that serves as the firm's corporate headquarters.

1970s

1970
Booz Allen goes public; 500,000 shares are sold to the public at $24 per share.

Allen retires, Bowen becomes chairman, and James W. Taylor becomes president.

1973
James Farley becomes president.

1975
Farley becomes chairman and Jack Lesher is appointed president.

1976
Booz Allen moves its corporate headquarters to New York.

In the largest-ever leveraged buyout involving a consulting firm, Booz Allen's partners buy back the stock, returning the firm to a private ownership with a new governance structure and a five-year plan for business development.

1977
Sales exceed $100 million.

1979
Booz Allen begins work with Chrysler Corporation, helping the automaker accomplish its historic turnaround.

The certificate for Booz Allen's public stock, traded between 1970 and 1976.

1980s

1980
Booz Allen publishes *Outlook*, the first in a series of management magazines.

1982
A Booz Allen vice president in the London office, Keith Oliver, develops the concept for supply chain management, working with Dutch electronics giant Philips.

1985
Mike McCullough is elected chairman.

The Düsseldorf office begins to spearhead a renewal of energy and investment in Europe, particularly in Germany, Austria, and Switzerland.

1986
Booz Allen initiates the Professional Excellence Awards.

1988
Staff exceeds 3,500.

1990s

1991
William Stasior is elected chairman and CEO.

Booz Allen reorganizes into the Worldwide Commercial Business (WCB), serving primarily the corporate sector, and the Worldwide Technology Business (WTB), serving primarily government clients.

1992
Booz Allen opens its new corporate headquarters on its own campus in McLean, Virginia.

Allen dies at the age of 88.

1993
The Worldwide Commercial Business adopts a new strategy known as Vision 2000.

1994
The Worldwide Technology Business adopts a new strategy following its own Vision 2000 process.

Former U.S. Secretary of State Henry Kissinger spoke with, left, Dan Lewis and, center, Cyrus Freidheim Jr., at a 1996 Booz Allen advisory board meeting.

Booz Allen looks to China as a source of growth. Shanghai's Oriental Pearl Tower, left, the world's third-largest television tower, is a symbol of the country's emergence as an economic power.

2000s

1995
Staff exceeds 6,000.

Booz Allen's magazine of thought leadership, *strategy+business,* begins publication.

1997
Sales exceed $1.3 billion

1999
Ralph W. Shrader, having been elected the previous year, takes office as chairman and CEO.

Booz Allen acquires Carta Corporate Advisors, the leading Nordic management consulting firm.

Worldwide offices exceed 100.

2000
Staff exceeds 10,000. Sales exceed $2 billion.

2001
The firm streamlines its name to Booz Allen Hamilton; adopts a new business definition ("global strategy and technology consulting firm") and a new, one-phrase mission ("Booz Allen Hamilton works with clients to deliver results that endure").

Engagements increasingly draw upon the combined capabilities of the firm's Worldwide Commercial Business and Worldwide Technology Business experts.

2002
Booz Allen publishes its first annual report on CEO turnover at the world's 2,500 largest publicly traded corporations.

2003
Booz Allen acquires Gemini Consulting Japan, doubling the size of the Tokyo office.

Booz Allen develops the OrgDNA online self-assessment tool, enabling company leaders to better understand how the inherent traits of their organizations influence employee behavior and affect company performance.

2004
Staff grows to 15,000. Sales reach $2.7 billion.

Booz Allen announces a three-year agreement to sponsor the Professional Golf Association's Washington, D.C.-area tournament under the name Booz Allen Classic.

Berlin's Brandenburg Gate is the symbol of freedom and unity in Germany, one of Booz Allen's strongest markets.

"Booz Allen Hamilton works with clients to deliver results that endure"

Index

Bold listings indicate illustrated material.

Author's Biography

Art Kleiner is a writer specializing in business management, inter-active media, corporate environmentalism, scenario planning, and organizational learning. He is the author of *Who Really Matters: The Core Group Theory of Power, Privilege, and Success*, which was named as one of the best business books of the year by Soundview Executive Book Summaries and HR.Com. He is also the author of *The Age of Heretics: Heroes, Outlaws and the Forerunners of Corporate Change*. With George Roth, research director of the MIT Center for Organizational Learning in the mid-1990s, Kleiner co-created a pioneering form of organizational story-telling, the "learning history"; Roth and Kleiner published two such histories with Oxford University Press: *Car Launch* and *Oil Change*.

Kleiner's column, "Culture and Change," appears regularly in *strategy+business*, the quarterly management magazine pub-lished by Booz Allen Hamilton, and he has also profiled leading management thinkers for the magazine. Kleiner is the editorial director of the best-selling *Fifth Discipline Fieldbook* series, co-authored with Peter Senge; titles include *The Fifth Discipline Fieldbook*, *The Dance of Change*, and *Schools That Learn*. Since 1987, he has taught courses on scenario planning and writing for new media at New York University's Interactive Telecommunications Program.

Kleiner is a research associate with Dialogos, a small, innovative consulting firm based in Cambridge, Massachusetts. He is the co-inventor of "Stepping Stones," a well-regarded leadership-development program for small- and moderate-budget organizations. Kleiner has also conducted week-long sessions at the Authentic Leadership conference conducted by the Shambhala Institute in Halifax, Nova Scotia. Kleiner lives near New York City, and maintains an ongoing web site of writing and perspective at http://www.artkleiner.com.

The Core Values of Booz Allen Hamilton

As a firm and as individuals, Booz Allen has committed to these core values, which express the principles that have guided the firm across 90 years. They were codified recently, under Ralph Shrader's leadership, to capture the firm's long-standing commitment to ethical conduct in how we treat one another as individuals and how we relate to our clients.

Business values

Client Service
Keeping client's mission the priority
Holding client value as the driver of service delivery
Defining own value by the value provided to clients
Doing what is best for the client

Diversity
Maintaining an inclusive work environment
Selecting and retaining diverse staff
Leveraging the differences of staff

Excellence
Going beyond the current standards
Developing high quality intellectual capital
Giving best effort all the time
Constantly striving for improvement

Entrepreneurship
Creating new value for the firm and its clients
Inspiring shared vision
Creating excitement to take action

Teamwork
Interacting collaboratively
Sharing knowledge, skills, success, and failure
Sharing vision and common objectives
Resolving conflicts professionally

Individual values

Professionalism
Challenging work that creates learning
Personal development and improvement
Demonstrating skills in effective ways

Fairness
Objectivity, managing by fact
Impartiality
Consistent application of agreed-upon criteria
Inclusiveness in work processes

Integrity
Adhering to firm's ethics
Requiring and modeling ethical behavior
Consistency in what we say and do
Representing the truth

Respect
Sensitivity to many perspectives and situations
Treating others impartially and with dignity
Listening
Granting legitimacy to other points of view

Trust
Reliability and sincerity in interactions
Keeping the best interests of clients, firm,
    team, and staff paramount
Not letting each other down

Booz Allen Hamilton's partners gathered during the firm's 90th-anniversary year.

Booz Allen Hamilton Officers *(October 2004)*

OFFICER	JOINED FIRM	OFFICER	JOINED FIRM	OFFICER	JOINED FIRM
John E. McGrath	August 30, 1963	Steven B. Wheeler	June 11, 1984	Thomas D. Williams	May 23, 1988
R. Keith Oliver	October 1, 1967	Natalie M. Givans	June 18, 1984	Vinay Couto	June 13, 1988
Joseph Nemec Jr.	May 11, 1970	John D. Lueders	July 9, 1984	Paul M. Doolittle	June 13, 1988
Gary D. Mather	January 1, 1972	Raul L. Katz	August 22, 1984	Lloyd W. Howell Jr.	July 18, 1988
Ralph W. Shrader	April 22, 1974	Reginald Van Lee	August 27, 1984	Vanessa M. Wallace	August 1, 1988
John F. Mulhern	January 6, 1975	Peter B. Mensing	September 1, 1984	William C. Jackson	August 22, 1988
Cornwell G. Appleby	November 1, 1975	Laurene A. Gallo	November 19, 1984	Charles L. Teschner Jr.	September 1, 1988
Fred L. Cipriano	March 15, 1976	Donald J. Vincent	April 1, 1985	Peter Bertone	September 12, 1988
Theodore M. Shema	September 1, 1976	Charles El-Hage	April 13, 1985	Mark J. Moran	September 19, 1988
Michael P. Noonberg	November 1, 1976	David Karp	July 29, 1985	Teresa L. Bozzelli	September 26, 1988
Bruce A. Pasternack	December 20, 1976	Matthew G. McKenna	July 29, 1985	William H. Stewart	December 19, 1988
Heather L. Burns	May 16, 1977	Martin J. Bollinger	December 9, 1985	Timothy Jackson	February 6, 1989
Francis J. Henry Jr.	August 15, 1977	Ronald A. Hodge	December 9, 1985	Judith H. Dotson	February 20, 1989
Daniel C. Lewis	January 9, 1978	Christopher M. Kelly	January 6, 1986	Michael E. Foley	May 1, 1989
S. Anthony Bianco	December 4, 1978	Rolf W. Habbel	February 3, 1986	Frederick W. Knops III	May 15, 1989
W. Frank Jones	December 4, 1978	Cynthia L. Broyles	February 10, 1986	Edward Frey	June 5, 1989
Douglas G. Swenson	December 4, 1978	Sam M. Porgess	March 3, 1986	Dermot Shorten	June 12, 1989
Joyce C. Doria	January 8, 1979	Jeffrey J. Kibben	March 3, 1986	Ivan C. De Souza	June 20, 1989
Martin E. Leshin	April 23, 1979	Lee J. Falkenstrom	March 28, 1986	Peter Soliman	July 1, 1989
Paul A. Branstad	February 18, 1980	Carl R. Salzano	June 2, 1986	Harry Hawkes Jr.	August 22, 1989
Gary L. Neilson	June 13, 1980	Eric A. Spiegel	June 9, 1986	Christian Burger	September 1, 1989
Gary D. Ahlquist	July 28, 1980	Cesare Mainardi	September 8, 1986	David G. Knott	September 5, 1989
Gary M. Schulman	September 2, 1980	Leticia Costa	October 1, 1986	William A. Thoet	September 11, 1989
Donald G. Busson	May 4, 1981	Klaus Mattern	October 1, 1986	Charlie R. Jones	October 2, 1989
Glen R. Bruels	June 29, 1981	Molly Finn	October 27, 1986	Vaidyanathan Chandrashekhar	November 13, 1989
Joseph W. Mahaffee	November 2, 1981	Nicholas J. Kuttner	December 1, 1986	Paolo A. Pigorini	May 14, 1990
Gerald S. Adolph	November 30, 1981	Robert Schuyt	December 1, 1986	Patrick Béhar	July 2, 1990
Harry F. Quarls	February 1, 1982	Paul F. Kocourek	February 17, 1987	James C. Weinberg	July 31, 1990
Mark J. Gerencser	June 14, 1982	Michael C. Saunders	February 23, 1987	Thomas Künstner	August 13, 1990
Ghassan Salameh	July 12, 1982	René Perillieux	March 1, 1987	Thomas J. Mayor	August 13, 1990
Neil T. Gillespie	August 2, 1982	Thomas Hansson	March 9, 1987	Christian Fongern	September 1, 1990
Alonso Martínez	October 1, 1982	Francis Liu	April 23, 1987	Steven J. Veldhoen	September 1, 1990
Helmut Meier	October 1, 1982	Gilon Irwin	April 27, 1987	Giorgio Biscardini	September 3, 1990
David L. Newkirk	November 1, 1982	Viren Doshi	June 1, 1987	Adam Seale	September 3, 1990
Douglas M. Hardman	July 1, 1983	Jeffrey S. Tucker	June 12, 1987	Fernando Napolitano	September 10, 1990
George D. Tillmann	July 11, 1983	Gerd Wittkemper	July 1, 1987	Neil C. McArthur	September 17, 1990
Kenneth F. Wiegand Jr.	July 25, 1983	Gary C. Cubbage	July 20, 1987	Sarah Butler	September 26, 1990
Dennis O. Doughty	August 18, 1983	Evan R. Hirsh	July 20, 1987	Riccardo Lotti	October 1, 1990
Joseph E. Garner	September 1, 1983	Barratt H. Jaruzelski	August 24, 1987	Klaus-Peter Gushurst	January 1, 1991
Joanne S. Bessler	October 3, 1983	John B. Frelinghuysen	September 8, 1987	DeAnne M. Aguirre	January 14, 1991
Douglas E. Himberger	October 4, 1983	Bertrand Kleinmann	September 15, 1987	Claudia Staub	March 1, 1991
Charles Beever	January 6, 1984	Mark L. Herman	November 30, 1987	Charles P. Zuhoski	April 8, 1991
Patrick F. Peck	March 1, 1984	W. Foster Rich	December 7, 1987	Christopher Ling	April 15, 1991
Bertrand G. Shelton	April 2, 1984	Marco Kesteloo	May 16, 1988	Richard Hauser	May 1, 1991